KF 390.5 .C6 B678 2002

Brandt Graterol, Leopoldo

Evaluating web sites for legal compliance

DATE DUE

GAYLORD			PRINTED IN U.S.A.

Evaluating Web Sites for Legal Compliance

Basics for Web Site Legal Auditing

Leopoldo Brandt Graterol
and
John Ng'ang'a Gathegi

The Scarecrow Press, Inc.
Lanham, Maryland, and Oxford
2002

SCARECROW PRESS, INC.

Published in the United States of America
by Scarecrow Press, Inc.
A Member of the Rowman & Littlefield Publishing Group
4720 Boston Way, Lanham, Maryland 20706
www.scarecrowpress.com

PO Box 317, Oxford, OX2 9RU, UK

Copyright © 2002 by Leopoldo Brandt Graterol and John Ng'ang'a Gathegi

All rights reserved. No part of this publication may be reproduced, stored in a retrieval system, or transmitted in any form or by any means, electronic, mechanical, photocopying, recording, or otherwise, without the prior permission of the publisher.

British Library Cataloguing in Publication Information Available

Library of Congress Cataloging-in-Publication Data

Brandt Graterol, Leopoldo, 1965-
Evaluating web sites for legal compliance : basics for web site legal auditing / Leopoldo Brandt Graterol and John Ng'ang'a Gathegi.
p. cm.
Includes bibliographical references and index.
ISBN 0-8108-4473-7 (alk. paper)

1. Web sites—Law and legislation—United States. I. Gathegi, John Ng'ang'a. II. Title.
KF390.C6 B73 2002
343.7309'944—dc21 2002013519

∞™ The paper used in this publication meets the minimum requirements of American National Standard for Information Sciences—Permanence of Paper for Printed Library Materials, ANSI/NISO Z39.48-1992.
Manufactured in the United States of America.

Contents

Preface

From the assembling of the first Altair personal computer to the creation of the TCP/IP protocol, many remarkable events have occurred in the technological community. But no other event has marked the emergence of e-commerce and electronic communications like the development of the "server" concept by Tim Berners-Lee. Only an advanced concept like the server could have allowed thousands of users with different operating systems access to files in a single computer. Such a single computer may be linked to or communicate with millions of other computers. These other computers may be accessed by other third parties either directly or through linkings from yet other different computers around the world. The server concept was the seed of the web site as we know it today. Legal consequences of these links were barely considered at the beginning, and are just now taking on a critical importance.

Web sites are among new tools being reviewed and scrutinized by the legal community worldwide. Because of their structural *sui generis* nature, web sites can be analyzed and classified using various methodologies, which vary from revision of a single aspect to a deeper review of many of its elements. In sum, a rigid evaluation system is almost impossible. This is particularly so where the focus is from a worldwide legal perspective.

Due to lack of uniformity and a systematic methodology for analyzing web pages from a legal standpoint, we have designed a flexible evaluation system consisting of a modular structure that is applicable to any single page worldwide. Furthermore, the analysis or "audit" can be performed with tools available on the World Wide Web and, therefore, wherever there is a connection to the Internet

Our contribution to the legal and technological community aspires to provide some basic legal guidelines to anyone involved in the operation of web sites to prevent or reduce adverse legal consequences that may affect the performance of a business.

This book is not intended to provide legal advice. The reader in need of such advice should contact a competent attorney. The application of the legal evaluation system contained in this book will provide the reader with some hints and indications, but because legal systems differ among countries, and may also differ within a country at the state level, it may be prudent to retain competent local counsel. The audience for this book may include webmasters, directors of a company that owns a web site, or even middle management. It could also include the individual proprietor setting up a web site.

As will soon become apparent, due to the intricacies of the virtual environment, the potential liabilities for a web site owner could be endless. Thus, attempting to cover every legal aspect related to the digital environment is an impossible mission, even if we provided the reader with only a brief reference to every topic. This book therefore deals only with issues we deemed basic for the legal configuration of a web site, either already online, or at the planning stage, especially regarding the protection of the rights of the web site owner and the end user. The more complex cyberspace becomes, the larger the list of issues that will have to be addressed by other authors.

The structure of the auditing system presented here will allow the upgrade of all or any of the elements as technology evolves and the legal environment changes. We have included court decisions in the appendices so the reader may experience how the courts are grappling with some of the legal issues presented by the World Wide Web.

Chapter 1

A Due-Diligence Approach to Web Site Evaluation

The Need for Legal Evaluation: Basics of Legal Due Diligence

Before delving into the topic of this book, it is appropriate to clarify some aspects of the "due-diligence" process for the reader's benefit. The term due diligence is often used but hardly understood. Legal due diligence involves those tasks that a person or company would normally expect to perform to mitigate adverse legal effects of a planned activity, such as a company merger. A record of such undertaken tasks could later help to prove that due diligence and prudence were taken into consideration in a given situation. Thus, due diligence from our perspective involves assessing any potential legal situation that may negatively affect the operations of a web site or web activity.

Such an assessment will be vital for companies which conduct business on the Internet. This was well illustrated during the "dot-com" crisis of 2001, an event that undoubtedly affected companies with unduly configured web sites, from the legal point of view. Despite the crisis, a substantial number of businesses are migrating to a solely online presence, and traditional businesses have adopted the Internet as an everyday tool for doing businesses. From insurance companies, portals, e-commerce sites, to government and federal agencies sites, they all will require compliance with some basic legal principles, in addition to any applicable legally binding legislation in a particular country. Of course, it is difficult to prevent or be aware of each and every detail legally affecting a web site, or even keep up to date with relevant legislation.

The basic conclusion here is that some sort of flexible approach or methodology is required. This may be developed from scratch or based upon an existing framework, but in the end some form of evaluation or auditing will be necessary to assess the legal risks affecting the web site.

Due diligence requires that web sites be reviewed to identify situations that might potentially legally affect the web site, assess the legal implications and measure the risks, and take any necessary action or make corrections to mitigate or eliminate such risks.

It is easily evident that a due-diligence process can become a difficult matter in any environment. It becomes even harder in the online environment, where there are uncertainties such as: the identity of a message's author, message integrity (one is not certain that the message has been received intact or it has been altered in transit), and the likelihood of repudiation of message authorship. Given the phenomenal growth of web activity discussed above, one can easily imagine the scope of the problem.

where there are uncertainties such as: the identity of a message's author, message integrity (one is not certain that the message has been received intact or it has been altered in transit), and the likelihood of repudiation of message authorship. Given the phenomenal growth of web activity discussed above, one can easily imagine the scope of the problem.

It is clear then that aspects found only in the online world must be carefully reviewed and analyzed holistically in order to provide an adequate guide on how to proceed to prevent negative legal consequences. The goal of an effective evaluation cannot be achieved if there is no clear definition of the extent of the legal consequences that are being evaluated or mitigated. The extent of the legal consequences is determined by the scope of each dot-com project. Accordingly, the legal aspects deriving from a dot-com project cannot be specifically determined and their extent delimited if the magnitude of the project has not been set. At least four questions must be asked:

1. What is the legal framework under which the project is to be developed?
2. What is the geographical scope of the project?
3. What is the time frame to accomplish the legal diligence required?
4. What are the economic resources allocated in the budget to the legal tasks?

These are just basic considerations. Effective evaluation of the legal aspects of an Internet project and the corresponding web site may not be achieved if the minimum parameters have not been defined.

Characteristics of the Analytical Tool

The need for a flexible approach to the legal evaluation of a web site has made it necessary to devise a due-diligence procedure that is also flexible. The flexibility is achieved by way of a modular design, taking into account the strategies described below.

Modular Structure

Our web legal evaluation system is composed of modules or sections whose number may be increased or reduced according to the need of each project. The beginning structure is made up of seven basic modules: domain names module, intellectual property module, hypertext links agreements and related contracts module, conditions of use and commercial terms module, privacy policy module, spam policy module, and security module. Additional modules may be added to examine other aspects that may be necessary, depending on the nature of the service to be provided from the site, or as required by the changing technologies.

Web Uniformity

Because of its structure, our web evaluation system may be applied to any single web site worldwide, regardless of language or country. The fact that each web page is composed of certain standard elements helps in this process.

Web Dependability

All the activities necessary to conduct the evaluation process may be made through tools available on the Internet. Information to review country-specific government or administrative regulations is even available online for some countries.

Ease of Use and Understanding

While the results from the evaluation system may require a deeper analysis in certain areas of the law, they will indicate some of the possible legal contingencies and remedies required. These recommendations are easy to understand and implement by professionals with expertise in the sector.

Chapter 2

The Analytical Structure

Preliminary Test of Web Site Content

The structure of our web legal evaluation system is comprised of several stages. At the outset, a set of questions are asked as to the nature of the activity, the business purposes, as well as any other relevant information that may be required to fully understand the philosophy of the company whose web site is being evaluated. We call this the preliminary test. It is the only way to be fully involved in the process and be acquainted with what is to be assessed.

These basic issues can be categorized in the following groups:

1. Type of online presence: This is to determine the type of activity carried out at the web site. For example, is it merely an information site, or is it also involved in e-commerce? Who are the stakeholders (i.e., suppliers, clients), what is the nature of the transactions at the site (e.g., purchase versus subscription), and what are the security precautions of the site? For example, are the transactions encrypted?
2. Ownership of the information in the site: Who owns the web content (e.g., the webmaster, users, clients)? Is the content accurate?
3. Security in activities: Has the web owner adopted the applicable security measures for the material or activities to be performed at the site, such as payment, sending of confidential information, résumés, profiles, etc?
4. Legal compliance: Has the web owner complied with the applicable laws regarding taxes, advertising, sweepstakes, lotteries, gaming, and so on? Does the content violate any laws or commercial customs?

Once the above information is collected, the web site may be submitted to the modular evaluation of its components for a more thorough analysis.

Drafting Terms, Conditions, and Policies for Web Sites

The modular system deals mainly with drafting of terms, conditions, and policies. These have a purpose in the development of a site. They control the relationship between the site and navigating third parties, whether directly or indirectly. Online site terms, conditions, and policies are similar to those in the offline world. Legal terms reflect codes and regulations of the applicable laws, relating to such things as jurisdiction, copyright, and trademarks. They also include terms governing commercial relationships, such as consumer rights and obligations. Statements reflecting the firm's existing privacy policy should be included in the web site.

Drafting the general conditions for a web site should not be an onerous task. Any manager or employee may be able to draft or contribute to the commercial issues, while the legal counsel will review the legal issues. When a site is designed to be accessed from different countries using different languages, the legal implications become more complex. Even if the basic commercial terms consistently apply, the same provisions may be interpreted differently depending on the country and its laws.

In general, users rarely pay much attention to terms and conditions. They are vaguely aware of their relevance and sometimes even their content. Even fewer bother to read the terms, and may even leave a web site if they are forced to read the terms and conditions before they can proceed.

Web sites should clearly state the subject (e.g., legal terms, privacy policy) in the links in a specific manner, whenever possible using additional wording that explains the content of the links, even if it sounds obvious. The graphics and location of the links also require some thought. Ultimately, however, as more and more users become educated as to the legal implications of web sites, users will be looking for those legal terms and other conditions, wherever they are located on a page.

There is no particular formula for drafting terms, conditions, or policies. It is advisable to first decide on the main principles to be included. Using common sense is essential. One should think from the perspective of a user navigating a web site. What would you as a user expect to find?

Working with a web designer is of course a wise choice. Once the main principles for the conditions, terms, and policies of a web site have been established, they should be compared with those actually used by the web site owner's firm. This examination should cover commercial, legal, consumer protection, privacy, and any other relevant aspect. The idea is to prevent contradictions between what the firm does in the offline world and what it does in the online world.

Assuming there is no apparent contradiction between the offline and online practices of the firm, the next step is to set priorities and write them down. Consider how items included may affect the user or the firm. Using the list of priorities, one may now proceed to delimit each of the sections on terms, conditions, or policies as appropriate. This preliminary draft would then be reviewed with legal counsel for content and legal compliance. A comparison with competing firms on how they have addressed the issues might be instructive. Beware of copying and pasting from other sites, since no single model fits all business situations.

A Word about Licensing

One of the words that will be repeatedly mentioned in this book is "licensing." A license is permission granted by the owner of a right to other parties to use the property licensed. Within the context of this book, a license agreement is the contract by which the owner of any type of intellectual property allows someone else to use, sell, or sublicense the intellectual property in exchange for a sum of money or other consideration, such as sharing benefits derived from the license itself.

Licensing in this context involves rights to various types of intellectual property, such as inventions, trademarks, patents, industrial design, artistic and literary work, and music. In licensing, property rights of the item licensed remain with the owner. The licensee is obligated to use the license within the terms and conditions of the license agreement.

Businesses developing a web site might contract out certain services, such as the use of a search engine and the use of shopping cart technology. However, certain other elements of a web page, because of strategic or marketing reasons, cannot and should not be contracted out.

Many different licenses may be involved at any one time. With an Internet purchase, for example, the web site may be using licenses for identity, use of data bases, inventory control, secure certificates, sublicensing case management software, e-mail and instant messenger services, as well as other administrative programs. This means that management teams and legal departments must coordinate the licensing process and keep the nature of the business in focus.

Licensing with Latest Technology

Licensing has come online. Negotiating parties can have access to secure conference rooms online where they are able to negotiate license agreements, discuss the drafts, make the necessary amendments, and even chat in an electronically secure environment.[1] A variety of legal forms are also available for the parties to save time and money. Such sites, like many domain names registrars, offer an escrow service for storage and ultimate transfer of physical assets once the transaction is complete. Moreover, in the case of patents that cover validity and enforceability, insurance policies are available.

Web Site Evaluation

Domain Names Module

Domain names are intimately related to intellectual property issues. However, they are also considered an independent topic worthy of an independent analysis. Because of their importance, we address domain names here as an aspect separate from the intellectual property module.

A domain name is a customized electronic address that references an individual set of Internet protocols (IP). The IP number enables a computer host to locate a remote computer. Each domain name (and IP) must be unique.[2] A domain name is a user-friendly replacement for the sets of numbers that actually locate a computer; it gets the Internet user to a specific web site. The name may also hint at the contents of the site.

As the cases we have included in the appendices illustrate, the topic of domain names is probably one of the most complex and interesting in the Internet arena. We will cover here only some basic aspects that the web site must comply with. As discussed above, a domain name is the alphanumeric combination by which a web site can be located (e.g., www.web.com). When one types in a web address name, the DNS or domain name server translates the name into an IP address. Different servers locate the web page and retrieve it for the requesting user. The Internet Corporation for Assigned Names and Numbers (ICANN) is the entity in charge of all matters relating to domain names.

ICANN, a non-profit corporation put together by a coalition of Internet user communities in business, academic institutions, and technical users, was established in October 1998. With government recognition, ICANN coordinates the technical management of the Internet's domain name system, allocates IP addresses, assigns protocol parameters, and manages the root server system.

There are various types of domain names. The so-called top-level domain names (TLD) include ".com", ".net", ".org", ".cc", ".tv", ".biz", ".info", ".edu", ".mil", as well as the country code top-level domains (CCTLD), such as .com.ve (Venezuela); .com.ar (Argentina); .com.br (Brazil). The domains were originally designed to signify specific organizations. For example, .com would be used by commercial organizations, .org by non-profit organizations, .edu by educational institutions, and .mil for the military. Except for the military and to a lesser extent the educational institutions, this special significance has all but disappeared, with organizations attempting to cover all bases when registering a domain name.

Domain name registration may be made through any of the approved and ICANN-authorized registrars, and can generally be done online. All the names and web sites registered can be linked directly from the ICANN web site. The number of domain name registrations increases every week, and tariffs for domain registration are falling down, as more new registrars apply and are authorized each year.

Details for domain name registration procedures in specific countries can be found at the web site of the responsible entity in each country, i.e., the Network Information Center (NIC) of each country. For example, this would be nic.ve for Venezuela; nic.pe for Perú, and so on. This information can be accessed from the ICANN web site. In the United States, Network Solutions is probably the most popular domain name registrar.

It is advisable to register the domain name in each country in which a company plans to conduct business. Some companies go even further and request the domain in all countries. This is mainly to prevent another party or a competitor from rerouting a web site to a different URL (uniform resource locator), whose content may be illegal or may harm the image of the web site. However, one should be aware of restrictions imposed by each country. Some countries request the establishment of a physical entity, and others require the billing contact to be a resident. It is best to check the NIC of each country to determine the limitations in each case. Even in cases where there are no limitations, for example where one can register online, it is advisable to have a local attorney make the application and handle the payment of the fees directly. In the long run, effective legal management can often save more money than the "do-it-yourself" approach.

As the cases in the appendices illustrate, courts in certain countries, like the United States, have already had to deal with issues such as bad-faith registration of domain names and abuse of the process. Even for countries having no legislation in this area, local NIC offices have set up a system for the submission of registration disagreements to dispute resolution procedures. This is assuming that the specific country will legally recognize such procedures. Consulting a local attorney would be a good idea. A cardinal rule, especially for a dot-com company, is to obtain a domain name before launching a major project anywhere in the world. If a domain name has already been taken, the better strategy is to purchase it from the registrant, rather than trying litigation. One may also use an expedited procedure like the Uniform Dispute Resolution Policy, approved by ICANN and accepted by the registrant when requesting a domain name.

While the majority of the local NIC offices have conformed their domain name registration agreements to the ICANN Uniform Dispute Resolution Policy, the option of going to court is still available to the aggrieved party. It should be noted, however, that in many cases the registration agreements have clauses that unilaterally allow the registering entity to revoke the registration of a given domain name due to trademark violations or if inaccurate or false information was supplied during the registration process.

Intellectual Property Module

This module covers both first-generation intellectual property (trademarks, copyright, and patents) and second-generation intellectual property (deep linking, framing, and meta-tagging) and tries to provide some ideas as to how to detect IP legal needs and potential contingencies.

A web site should indicate ownership of all copyrights, trade secrets, patents, or other intellectual property rights at the site, except for those rights held by others, with specific prohibition on disassembling, decompiling, reverse engineering, or otherwise deriving source code from the software. Also prohibited will be unauthorized reproduction, distribution, publication, licensing, modification, creation of derivative works, transfer, selling, renting or leasing of information, software products, or services from the site.

First-Generation IP: Trademarks

A trademark includes any name, symbol, or device of any combination used or intended to be used in commerce to identify and distinguish the goods of one manufacturer or seller from goods manufactured or sold by others, and to indicate the sources of the goods. In short, a trademark is a brand name. A service mark identifies and distinguishes the services of one provider from services provided by others and indicates the source of the services. A certification mark is used in commerce with the owner's permission by someone other than its owner, to certify regional or other geographic origin, material, mode of manufacture, quality, accuracy, or other characteristics of someone's goods or services, or that the work or labor on the goods or services was performed by members of a union or other organization.[3]

Trademark registration is not necessary. However, registration in the case of the United States has several advantages, including notice to the public of the registrant's claim of ownership of the mark, a legal presumption of ownership nationwide, and the exclusive right to use the mark on or in connection with the goods or services set forth in the registration. Domestic registration can also be used as basis for obtaining registration in foreign countries.[4]

All the related aspects of intellectual property must be properly protected by filing before a trademark or copyright office, not only in the country of origin but also in the other countries where the trademarks are to be used. It is important to consider the cost of registering or filing applications of trademarks in various countries.

A trademark may consist of multiple filings, as many as the classes to be protected. Because there may be a number of classes involved in the operation, it can be a very expensive task that may affect the cash flow of a project, if not considered. Normally the law firm handling the corporate aspects of a project will contact their correspondent law firms in those countries where filing is necessary. Your law firm should closely supervise these corresponding law firms. It is important to consider any other expenses or legal fees related to the filing process in the different countries, including legalization, assignment of trademarks if not requested by the owner, and writs to consign power of attorney, often presented after the filing has been made.

The client has to be careful not make unnecessary trademark searches either through online means or by using local law firms in every country, since the requests are usually seen by third parties. This can happen on the Internet or even by officers of the local patent and trademark office. These third parties might file for registration of the trademark whose search is being requested, because they can tell from the results that the trademark is available.

It is also advisable that the requesting company be incorporated prior to owning the trademarks. The power of attorney authorizing your trademark local counsel in the different countries should be granted in advance. Late presentation of this document may cause additional expenses for late filing of the document before the local trademark office.

The company may even supervise the status of the trademark applications, in the United States, by using the search engine supplied by the United States Patent and Trademark Office, or may do so worldwide by means of the different paid systems available, such as www.trademarks.com or www.demarcas.com (for Latin American counties).

There are many classes for the filing of trademarks, and the reader may wonder whether filing is needed on each and every class. It is not always clear how the protection works. For example, if one is running a start-up, the most probable class to apply for would be Class 38, which covers telecommunications services. This class will provide protection if one wants to advertise the project on television, the Internet, radio, or even in magazines. One does not have to file an application in a class that covers magazines or publications unless the purpose of the project is publishing or an advertising agency.

There are, however, extreme cases where a company spends enormous amounts of money in applications, to prevent anyone from applying for a particular trademark, regardless of the class, and later on, alleges an existing right. There is always a risk of someone filing a cancellation action for nonuse of the trademark, if many applications are made and are not used.

Copyright

Copyright is a form of protection provided by law to authors of "original works of authorship," including literary, dramatic, musical, artistic, and certain other intellectual works. This protection is available to both published and unpublished works.[5]

Copyright law generally gives the owner of a work the exclusive right to do and to authorize others to do the following:

- To reproduce the work in copies or phonorecords;
- To prepare derivative works based upon the work;
- To distribute copies or phonorecords of the work to the public by sale or other transfer of ownership, or by rental or lease;
- To perform the work publicly, in the case of literary, musical, dramatic, and choreographic works, pantomimes, and motion pictures and other audiovisual works;
- To display the copyrighted work publicly, in the case of literary, musical, dramatic, and choreographic works, pantomimes, and pictorial, graphic, or sculptural works, including the individual images of a motion picture or other audiovisual work; and in the case of sound recordings, to perform the work publicly by means of a digital audio transmission.[6]

The protection of the copyright extends also to derivative works. Copyright protection exists from the time of work is created in fixed form.[7]

The posting of a copyright notice in a work and even in a web site, although not mandatory in some jurisdictions, is advisable to inform the public. The copyright is often designated with the symbol © or the word "copyright." Also included is the name of the author or an abbreviation by which the owner's name can be recognized and the year of first publication.

One should be on guard for copyright violations. There is a common belief that everything posted on the Internet grants automatic permission to freely reproduce copies. In fact, every posting on the Internet should be assumed to be copyrighted and a clearance from the author required, unless the contrary is specifically indicated.

A defense widely used in the case of copyright violation allegations is the concept of "fair use," which basically allows the use of parts of a copyrighted work for columnists, news articles, educational and similar works, without the author's permission. In fair use, no harm should be inflicted to the commercial value of the copied work. The fair use concept may not exist in some countries, therefore care must be taken when using this doctrine as a defense.

Patents

A patent for an invention is the grant of a property right to the inventor, issued by a Patent and Trademark Office. In the United States, the term of a new patent is twenty years from the date on which the application for the patent was filed or, in special cases, from the date an earlier related application was filed, subject to the payment of maintenance fees. Patent grants are effective only within territories in which they are registered.[8]

A patent allows one to prohibit others from making, using, selling, offering for sale, or importing into the granting country the patented article for a period of up to twenty years from the date of filing the application. The invention must be new, useful, and non-obvious. Typically inventions are aesthetic designs, functional items, functional methods, or asexually reproduced plants. Patents were designed to reward persons with a monopoly for particular benefits provided to the government and the people. Originally, "benefit" was loosely defined and the monopoly was not well connected to the benefit provided. In time the "benefit" to be offered became more narrowly defined to require a teaching about something unknown.[9]

A solid strategy is a must for any inventor. Typical concerns for individual inventors include cost, protection afforded, and strength of protection. These factors interact to provide several distinct strategies as outlined further below. Various legal tools provide protection, which principally depend upon priority dates and the importance of such a date. A priority date is the date a patent application is filed in accordance with particular statutory requirements. The priority date only applies to the disclosure contained in the application, making it imperative to have a complete disclosure. All or nearly all non-U.S. countries require that the priority date precede the first public disclosure or offer for sale. The United States requires the priority date to be within one year of the first public disclosure or offer for sale.[10]

Second-Generation IP: Linking

Links are points of connection, mainly in HTML (Hypertext Markup Language) format, that are included in web sites to drive users from one page to another and vice versa. Links on a page are usually indicated by the use of different font colors, underlines, block texts, or graphics. Sometimes there will be nothing to indicate a link, but a change from an arrow pointer to "hand" symbol whenever a cursor is over a linked item. Deep linking is linking to a page on another site other than the home page.

Some companies do not mind links to their sites—even using their trademarks. But they do mind deep links into their site. Why? Most home pages are the place where the most expensive banner advertisements appear, and for right now, the major income for Internet sites is in advertising dollars. There have been a few lawsuits involving deep linking. They have been mostly settled between the parties, so there is no real legal guidance for businesses at the moment. As the cases in the appendices illustrate, some of these lawsuits have been based upon trademark infringement, while others also include a violation of unfair competition laws. Unfair competition laws vary from state to state. In general, they prohibit a company from obtaining an unfair advantage by wrongful conduct. [11]

Whenever possible, links and deep links should be governed by an agreement between the parties, especially delineating the responsibilities of the party providing the deep linking to the linked party.

Framing

Framing refers to the capability of a browser to display various windows containing content of other web pages for various purposes. Sometimes the content will be to other web sites, necessitating permission requests to the owners.

In creating a web site, framing is the use of multiple independently controllable sections on a web presentation. This effect is achieved by building each section as a separate HTML file and having a "master" HTML file identify all of the sections. When a user requests a web page that uses frames, the result of the request is that multiple HTML files are returned, one for each visual section. Links in one frame can request another file that will appear in the same or another frame. A typical use of frames is to have one frame containing a selection menu in one frame and another frame that contains the space where the selected (linked to) files appear.

Framing can have copyright violation implications. The user, unless he is an expert in web pages design, may not easily tell which part of the displayed windows originates in which page, thus causing confusion in the general public as to the origin of the content. The web site should inform the user as to the origin of information, and the web site owner should periodically check for illegal framing.

Meta-Tagging

Meta-tags are special HTML tags that provide information about a web page. Unlike normal HTML tags, meta-tags do not affect how the page is displayed. Instead, they provide information such as who created the page, how often it is updated, what the page is about, and which key words represent the page's content. [12]

Typically, the "dream-come-true" of a web-site owner is to find its web site among the first ten results of a search engine request. Many search engine companies make promises in this respect, with varying results, sometimes with the site never showing up in the search results.

There are various factors determining the order of appearance of the web site results on a search engine request. Programming with HTML provides the ability to include specific tags that manage information displays to users. Meta-tags can also be used to index web pages and to improve the results of search engines by the inclusion of keywords within the site programming. Keywords may include names of company products. When a user requests a search, the search engine "reads" these keywords and determines that the page is about these words.

Not all search engines use keywords to prioritize searches. However, keywords used in meta-tags will usually have an effect on the ranking of a document by a search engine.

Normally the keyword included in the meta-tags refers to the main activity of the site. To prevent unnecessary legal exposure it is better not to mention any third parties' trademarks in the meta-tags.

Hypertext Link Agreements and Related Contracts Module

This section deals with the contractual relationships derived from or related to the operation of the web site. For a better understanding of the various types of existing contracts, we have divided the types of agreements in two categories.

Material Contracts

These are directly or indirectly involved in the web site, and include design, hosting, advertising brokerage, and search engine contracts. These agreements are mostly written and executed offline. These contracts may also include banner brokerage agreements, content development, icon agency agreements, and e-commerce application agreements. Although each contract governs a specific situation, it is advisable to negotiate, when possible, uniform legal terms favorable to the client. The use of similar terms in all the agreements will save time and prevent confusion when addressing an issue among many different agreements.

Hypertext link agreements are activated whenever a user clicks on a link in any given web page. Although it is not always clear to the user what the source of a linked element is, the fact is that the larger the number of links, the greater the legal risk for the web site. Unfortunately there is only one way to evaluate the impact of each link upon the web site: by "clicking" on each and every single link in the web page. Any given link is a path for users to a web site and its services. Thus, on the one hand are those users and parties that are legally contracted with the web site, through regular or electronic contracts called "clickwrap agreements." On the other hand are third party users who access and leave the web site, not even using any of the services available. Whatever the type of contract used, it should contain special provisions regarding web site activity.

Internet agreements have peculiarities not found in other common agreements. Some jurisdictions do not fully legally recognize electronic records, including electronic agreements. In such jurisdictions, therefore, the written agreement remains the single option to establish the existence of the conditions discussed and agreed upon by the parties. Specialized legal counsel in each jurisdiction should review every type of contract. Third parties having no previous contractual relationship with the web site become bound by the terms and conditions included in the web site once they have accessed the site.

There are many important elements to be considered in a contract, such as the nature of the relationship governed by the hypertext agreement (whether commercial, promotional, or informational); the rights and obligations of each party, including who controls what; ownership of the shared elements and licenses when necessary; performance conditions (these are almost always not even considered until a disastrous event occurs); data collection and information sharing; and each party's covenants and warranties.

Another important aspect to consider when reviewing links is conducting a search of links from the web site out to the Internet. This is to check every single site the web site is linked to and to determine also the legal conditions of the linked sites, and what potential damages this link may cause. Also check the links from the Internet into the web site. These may have been placed by a contractual relationship signed with other web sites, or by links placed in relevant search engines.

Link agreements are intimately related to the contractual strategy derived from the business model. The web site owners should know what the business model is since it is almost impossible to design a strategy if no business model has been defined.

Hosting Agreement

The hosting agreement should include a guaranteed bandwidth. A minimum guaranteed bandwidth will help evaluate one's site performance in peak periods and will test the performance of the hosting company to confirm that it is complying with the standards contained in the contract. At the beginning, what this minimum bandwidth is would be uncertain, but it is better to pay in excess than to have slow pages. Also, the agreement should include some sort of compensation or credit for the hours that your server has been down.

A crucial issue is the notification mechanism when the site is down. E-mail collected at another site is a good option. The hosting agreement should include terms for promptness and availability.

The contract must provide an emergency 1-800 number and an e-mail address to receive complaints in case of emergencies. It is convenient to include in the agreement that a copy of the complaint e-mail be sent to a good-faith third party, which may serve later to prove that the e-mail was timely sent. You may include in the contract the possibility of contract termination if as many as five com-plaints are sent and no response is obtained. This brings an evidentiary problem, but it is not impossible to prove in court by a variety of different means and records what has happened. Be sure to collect all the e-mails and faxes received from the hosting party since they may be useful in a judicial procedure.

The other issue involves relocating problems. Even where you have had a smooth commercial relationship with your hosting company, moving to a different hosting company is always a traumatic experience that should be planned in advance. A clause in the agreement with the old host should incorporate all available help when the site is moved, including access to the facilities, the support and the availability of all the technical material and manuals to move the site, and even a magnetic copy of the site itself in the last version uploaded online.

Another recommended clause is that the hosting company should not host companies that directly compete in the same market segment. Caution must be taken in this respect since the two web sites will be in the same server, and electronic manipulation may result in modification of information and, in the end, in damage for your web site. Most hosting parties are reluctant to agree, but it is indeed a reasonable request.

Conditions of Use and Commercial Terms Module

Terms or conditions refer to the obligations and rights of the web site owner and customer within a commercial relationship. Commercial terms are similar to commercial conditions in the offline world. A web site is only a different vehicle of doing business. Laws that rule regular commercial operations will apply accordingly. This is a fundamental module as it guides the user on how to navigate the web site and its links.

It is important to remember that there is no uniform set of terms and conditions that can be included in every web site. Terms and conditions will vary from industry to industry and from country to country, and should be designed to conform with the laws of a particular country.

In drafting conditions of use for web sites, it is useful to think like a user. For instance, what would the user expect from a web site? What can the user do or not do? What type of behavior is allowed or forbidden? The list can be long.

It is advisable to check out what competitors are doing on their web sites. This review may show competitive advantages or detect weaknesses in a web site design or legal structure.

Another good recommendation is to check the language in the different versions of your web site. Sometimes the wrong translation of a term or even a domain name may change a whole commercial strategy in a foreign country. Contacting legal counsel is advisable in this respect.

In some countries such as the United States, consumer protection laws are strictly enforced. Online advertising is a big issue in this context. Basic principles of the offline world generally apply to the online world as well. Many advertising laws, therefore, will be applicable to the online world. The main purpose of these kinds of laws is to prevent advertising from being misleading and deceptive. This means that the customer must be fully informed of the conditions and terms surrounding the commercial use of a web site.

To prevent an ad from being misleading and to ensure that consumers receive material information about the terms of a transaction, disclosures must be clear and conspicuous. In evaluating whether disclosures are likely to be clear and conspicuous in online ads, advertisers should consider the placement of the disclosure in an ad and its proximity to the relevant claim. Additional considerations include: the prominence of the disclosure, whether items in other parts of the ad distract attention from the disclosure, whether the ad is so lengthy that the disclosure needs to be repeated, whether disclosures in audio messages are presented in an adequate volume and cadence and visual disclosures appear for a sufficient duration, and whether the language of the disclosure is understandable to the intended audience.

To make a disclosure clear and conspicuous, advertisers should:

- Place disclosures near, and when possible, on the same screen as the triggering claim.
- Use text or visual cues to encourage consumers to scroll down a web page when it is necessary to view a disclosure.
- When using hyperlinks to lead to disclosures: make the link obvious; label the hyperlink appropriately to convey the importance, nature, and relevance of the information it leads to.
- Use hyperlink styles consistently so that consumers know when a link is available; place the hyperlink near relevant information and make it noticeable; take consumers directly to the disclosure on the click-through page; assess the effectiveness of the hyperlink by monitoring click-through rates and make changes accordingly.
- Recognize and respond to any technological limitations or unique characteristics of high tech methods of making disclosures, such as frames or pop-ups.
- Display disclosures prior to purchase, but recognize that placement limited only to the order page may not always work.
- Creatively incorporate disclosures in banner ads or disclose them clearly and conspicuously on the page the banner ad links to.
- Prominently display disclosures so they are noticeable to consumers, and evaluate the size, color, and graphic treatment of the disclosure in relation to other parts of the web page.
- Review the entire ad to ensure that other elements—text, graphics, hyperlinks, or sound—do not distract consumers' attention from the disclosure.
- Repeat disclosures as needed on lengthy web sites and in connection with repeated claims.
- Use audio disclosures when making audio claims, and present them in a volume and cadence so that consumers can hear and understand them.
- Display visual disclosures for a duration sufficient for consumers to notice, read, and understand them.
- Use clear language and syntax so that consumers understand the disclosures.

Legal Terms

A common question is whether there is a single set of legal terms for a web site that would have worldwide applicability. The answer would be no, since there will be as many types of legal terms as legal systems exist in the world. Countries have their own set of laws and regulations for cyberspace and therefore one needs to contact a local attorney in each jurisdiction. This is especially so where a firm has sizeable assets subject to seizure or other government sanctions.

An effective set of legal terms includes references to applicable laws, alternative dispute resolutions, the services to be offered by the web site, and the legal consequences for each party involved. It should also include any limitations or restrictions of liability or damages for any party. It should also indicate that acceptance of the terms of use is a condition of the use of the site and that use constitutes agreement to the terms.

Jurisdiction and Choice of Law

Jurisdiction and choice of law are key issues in any contractual relationship. Where the suit is filed matters, as does what the applicable law is. Jurisdiction and choice of law, therefore, are also two of the main concerns in the legal terms of a web site.

The selection of jurisdiction and choice of law for web pages as contractual obligations are just as important in the online world as they are in the offline world. Legal counsel would probably recommend choosing the most favorable jurisdiction, or choosing a jurisdiction where their clients have no assets to be seized.

Privacy Policy

Privacy terms or privacy policies are key issues in cyberspace. The privacy terms in a web site provide users with information related to data collected by the web site, either directly (forms, questionnaires) or indirectly (cookies, spiders). Among the main aspects covered by a privacy policy will be: (a) the type of information is collected and how it is collected, (b) what the site does with the information collected, and (c) with whom the web site shares this information. Privacy policies will be handled differently by different companies, even within the same sector.

Web-site owners confront a difficult decision—whether to certify their web sites by a third-party privacy seal or prepare a privacy policy on their own based on the internal information and privacy practices of the corporation. Needless to say, these two alternatives are not mutually exclusive. One may request a third-party privacy seal and build a privacy policy.

Users generally want to know that a web site they are visiting is concerned about their personal information and privacy. A variety of mechanisms are available to collect information from the public. Information is often gathered:

(a) at registration; (b) once the user has logged in, by the way of questionnaires; or (c) by allowing the users to have the webmaster's e-mail available and a contact e-mail address exclusively to deal with complains about privacy on the web site.

Whenever a user visits a web site, the site collects some information about that user. Such information may include the user's domain name or the last URL visited prior to visiting the particular web site. It will also include the user's IP address. Sites use this information to analyze visitor's activities by counting, tracking, and aggregating the traffic data to a site. Also, if a user enters a sweepstake or contest on a web-site, personally identifying information will usually be collected.

The collection tool having been chosen, the company needs to review what information must be in the questionnaire. As we mentioned above, privacy policies consider three basic aspects: what information is collected, what the site does with the information obtained, and with whom the site shares it. Therefore, the majority of the questions asked should be those related to these fundamental aspects.

A site should disclose its information gathering and dissemination practice for the visitor. A responsible site will give the user the choice of "opting out." This allows the user to opt out of receiving communications about new features or services from a web site.

"Cookies"

Cookies are pieces of data containing personal information that a web site transfers to a user's hard drive for record-keeping purposes. They usually store a user's preferences on a particular site, saving time, for example, on retyping frequently used information, such as log-ins. Cookies cannot store any personal information about the user that the user does not voluntarily supply to the web site. Cookies do not contain viruses. A server can only get data from the cookie it wrote to the cookie file—it cannot go fishing for information on the hard drive. Although many browsers are initially set up to accept cookies, a user can reset the browser to refuse some or all cookies. Refusing to accept cookies, however, may sometimes result in inaccessibility to some parts or features of a particular web site.

Cookies are one of the most widely used, misused, and misunderstood features of the web. Their basic function is simple: to allow web servers to store and retrieve information on the client side. Although cookies can make the web surfing experience more personalized and streamlined, many users regard them with suspicion because of concerns about privacy. When used appropriately, cookies can be an invaluable tool for a webmaster. You can use them to simplify sign-on procedures, set up shopping carts, and provide individual users with more personalized information on your site. Site visitors are becoming increasingly discriminating: they demand useful content presented quickly and clearly.

Whenever a web browser requests a file from the web server that sent it a cookie, the browser sends a copy of that cookie back to the server along with the request. Thus a server sends you a cookie and you send it back whenever you request another file from the same server. In this way, the server knows you have visited before and can coordinate your access to different pages on its web site. For example, an Internet shopping site uses a cookie to keep track of which shopping basket belongs to you. A server cannot find out your name, e-mail address, or anything about your computer using cookies.

Normally, cookies are only sent back to the server that originally sent them to the browser and to no one else. A server can set the domain attribute for a cookie so that any server in the same Internet subdomain as the computer that sent the cookie will have the cookie sent along with a file request. This is so those larger sites that utilize multiple servers can coordinate their cookies across all the servers.

Popular rumors about web cookies describe them as programs that can scan your hard drive and gather information about you including: passwords, credit card numbers, and a list of the software on your computer. None of this is close to the truth. The short of it is that a cookie is a short piece of data, not code, which is sent from a web server to a web browser when that browser visits the server's site. The cookie is stored on the user's machine, but it is not an executable program and cannot do anything to your machine. Web sites use cookies for a number of different reasons. Some of the most common include:

- Site Personalization: You can use cookies to identify visitors and direct them to areas of your site that might interest them most. This can be as simple as flagging new stories or products added to the site since their last visit or as complicated as rendering pages that are almost completely customized based on stored preferences (favorite music, nonfiction categories, etc.).
- Online Ordering: Many e-commerce sites use cookies to track additions or deletions to a shopping cart. Sites can use session cookies that are valid only for the duration of that particular visit, or design them so that users can return to the site days later and complete their transactions.
- Web Site Tracking: Cookies provide you with a more accurate count of site visitors and are thus useful for web site tracking. Using cookies, you can ensure that someone who visits your site three times per day is not counted as a unique user each time. You can also see how often repeat visitors visit and what items they view most often (very helpful if you want to personalize a site).[13]

In summary, a good privacy policy will clearly address several issues. It will explain why the web site needs the information it gathers and how it uses this information. It will state with whom it shares this information, and the need to share. It will also indicate how it gathers this information and where and how it stores it. It will provide a way for the user to remove or edit personal information collected by the web site, and an option of "opting out" of receiving communications from the web site about new features or services.

Spam Policy

The matter of spam is a serious one, more so for firms that do not have the technical or financial capacity to guard the system from unsolicited mail. In a nutshell, spam refers to unsolicited mail. A web site or some other person can not contact a user unless the user agrees otherwise or has invited the party to make a contact, either directly (a letter, for example) or indirectly (as in classified advertisement, for example). This has raised the issue of whether the e-mail addresses displayed in commercial or promotional web sites may be a target for commercial mail.

Spam terms inform the user what the web site's policy is regarding this annoyance. The spam issue may be addressed by a web site from three different perspectives:

1. Enforcing anti-spam policies within the web site; this is within the web site environment and the different communities that may be available such as, chats, bulleting boards, free e-mail, and video chat.
2. Enforcing anti-spam policies toward the different entities commercially engaged in activities with the web site such as web developers, employee consultants, and even registered users of a web site.
3. Compliance with the anti-spam applicable laws of the relevant country, such as including contact information and instructions on how a user can remove personal information. Compliance will vary depending on the scope of each regulation—the type of electronic commerce involved, for example, and the parties to which the legal obligations are addressed, such as the Internet service providers, commercial web sites, and others.

The drafting of anti-spam policies becomes a very important aspect of the activity of the web site. It shows the attitude of the web site sponsors toward the spam. Some sites even provide free anti-spam software for down-loading. They also provide e-mail addresses where they can receive letters, opinions, or complaints regarding spam within the web sites.

Security

While it is not mandatory for all web sites to provide secure communications, as a matter of "netiquette," web sites should be able to provide their users with some type of security system, either secure socket layers (SSL), secure electronic transactions (SET), encryption, or even secure certificates. SSL technology encrypts personal information, including passwords and credit card numbers to prevent the reading of the information while it is being transmitted. Antifraud systems for credit card operations should also be in place. We will not make any comment about firewalls since normally this is a responsibility of the hosting party. Suffice it to say that an e-commerce user who finds a non-secure transactions mode on a web site may not be inclined to return to that web page.

Notes

1. A service of this nature can be found at www.pl-x.com.

2. David C. Najarian, "Internet Domains and Trademark Claims: First Amendment Considerations," *Journal of Law & Technology* 41 (2001): 127.

3. Lori E. Simon, "Appellations of Origin: The Continuing Controversy," *Journal of International Law Business* 5 (1983): 132.

4. Marshall A. Leaffer, "The New World Of International Trademark Law," *Marquette Intellectual Property Law Review* 2 (1998): 1.

5. L. Ray Patterson, "Copyright in the New Millennium: Resolving the Conflict between Property Rights and Political Rights," *Ohio State Law Journal* 62 (2001): 703.

6. Andy Johnson-Laird, "Symposium: Copyright Owners' Rights and Users' Privileges on the Internet: The Anatomy of the Internet Meets the Body of the Law," *Dayton Law Review* 22 (1997): 465.

7. Norman Siebrasse, "A Property Rights Theory of the Limits of Copyright," *University of Toronto Law Journal* 51 (2001): 1.

8. Robert P. Merges, "Commercial Success and Patent Standards: Economic Perspectives on Innovation," *California Law Review* 76 (1988): 805.

9. Robert P. Merges and Richard R. Nelson, "On The Complex Economics Of Patent Scope," *Columbia Law Review* 90 (1990): 839.

10. Stephanie Gore, "Eureka! But I Filed Too Late: The Harm/Benefit Dichotomy of a First-to-File Patent System," *University of Chicago Law School Roundtable* (1993): 293.

11. See Deep Linking description at www.zdtv.com/zdtv/callforhelp/soho/jump/0,3652,2316841,00.html.

12. U. Paylago, "Trademark Infringement, Meta Tags, and the Initial Interest Confusion Remedy," *Media Law & Policy* 9 (2000): 49.

13. Teresa Scassa, "Text and Context: Making Sense of Canada's New Personal Information Protection Legislation," *Ottawa Law Review* 32 (2000/2001): 1.

Chapter 3

Toward Effective Drafting of Terms, Conditions, and Policies for Web Sites

At this point the reader may probably be asking: Why not just copy the terms, conditions of use, and policies of some other well-made web site? The answer to this is simple: Apart from possible copyright issues, the reader should be aware of some adverse consequences that can arise from this practice.

First, it is important to note that prior to drafting any type of conditions, terms, or policies for a web site, a careful examination of the business model must be conducted in order to fully understand what is being regulated.

Merely copying terms, conditions, or policies skips the essential step of the analytical process necessary to address the specific circumstances. Copied material might also contain errors and defective terms. Thus, the risk of copying and pasting conditions, terms, and policies may outweigh the cost of carefully drafting conditions, terms, and policies right from the start.

In addition to the points discussed above, terms and conditions will clearly indicate:

- What constitutes legitimate and illegitimate use.
- Age requirements where contractual relations are formed.
- The site's privacy policy.
- A warranty disclaimer for damage liability for inaccuracies, typographical errors, and suitability for use of products or services at the site.
- Disclaimer of liability for the user's infringement of intellectual property rights.
- Disclaimer of liability for the site's nonavailability for use.
- Disclaimer of liability for out-links leading to third-party sites.
- An indemnification clause for actions that exceed any agreed liability.
- Agreement by the user not to directly or indirectly export or reexport software to any countries that are subject to export restrictions.
- Jurisdiction and governing law.
- Assignment of rights.
- Reservation of right to modify terms.
- Severability clause preserving valid and enforceable provisions.
- Entirety of the agreement.

Web Diligence Checklist

The following checklists apply to both start-ups and ongoing projects.

The Project

Position: First determine the economic status of the company.

Scope: Determine the scope of the project (local, state, national, international).

Budget: Determine the budget that can be allocated for legal fees.

Services: Prepare the necessary agreements to be signed or discussed for the project development, including, for example, agreements for the web site hosting, consultants, and so on.

Web Auditing Process

With the above information and a good understanding of the purpose of the web site, you are now able to carry out a proper assessment of the legal needs of the web site. You should first define the necessary modules for analysis according to the modular system described in this book. Modules should at least include:

Domain Names
Intellectual Property
Privacy Policy
Conditions of Use and Commercial Terms
Legal Terms
Security

Domain Names Module

Determine the potential domain names for the project and register on each and every top-level domain (TLD) available: .com, .net, .org., .cc, .ws, .tv are a few examples. Also determine if there are plans for launching new domain names of this type by accessing, for example, ICANN and Network Solutions web sites.

Having determined the scope of the project, proceed to register the domain name. You may use any web service like Network Solutions to do this, or just contact a local attorney in countries where you need a country code extension (CCTLD).

Intellectual Property Module

Trademarks

Design a strategy to comply with all the IP aspects for your project. For trademarks, for example, hold a meeting with your trademark counsel and supply all the relevant information regarding your trademarks. Keep in mind that your trademark needs to be requested on each and every class belonging to the activity you are developing (e.g., you require protection on International Class 38 of Telecommunications if running a web site):

Grant the corresponding power of attorney for local and foreign counsels.

Carefully supervise trademark counsel by demanding periodic reports.

Copyrights

Check if you want to copyright the design of your web site. Also check all the content of your site and ask for the appropriate copyright permissions, if needed.

Patents

Check if you want to patent your business model, procedure, product, or idea that is to be available at your site, or if licensing of any type of patent will be necessary.

Second-Generation IP

Check the structure of the web site, specifically the level of interconnectedness and links that it has.

Hypertext Link Agreements and Related Contracts Module

Examine every link on your web site to determine its destination. Check if a contractual agreement is needed for any of the links. Do this every time the web site is revised and new links are added. Determine also which agreement your web site is going to operate with, electronic or print-based.

Check that vital agreements, such as web hosting and web development, are correctly drafted.

Conditions of Use and Commercial Terms Module

Review the operation of the web site and its scope, and tell the users what they need to know regarding its use. Review your product lines and clearly state conditions and warranties under which the products are offered, return policies, and money-back policies. Also review any consumer protection laws that may be applicable.

Checklist Items:

Terms of Use and Acceptance of Conditions
Member Conduct
Community Guidelines (Chat, E-mail, Clubs, Message Boards)
Standard Advertising Terms and Conditions
System Availability
Inventory
Sales Policy:

a) Defective Products
b) Overdue Delivery
c) Return Policies

Order Cancellations
Shipping
Payment and Taxes
Warranty

Privacy Policy Module

Review your company privacy policies, both offline and online. Using these policies and user input, draft a clear and concise privacy policy for your web site. You may want to allow users to access, modify, or delete any item in their personal information held by the web site.

Checklist Items:

What is the corporate privacy policy in the offline world?
What information is collected by the site and by what means?
Who collects the information?
How is the information used and with whom is it shared?
Cookies: How are they used?
What are the opt-in or opt-out mechanisms available to the users?
How can the user access, edit, or delete confidential personal information?
Is the site certified by a third-party seal?
Is there a contact to whom privacy concerns may be addressed?
Is there a specific person charged with enforcing the privacy policy?
Will the user be able to participate in reviewing the policy?

Legal Terms Module

Make a list of all the relevant legal information that you want to make available to the users in this section of the web site. Place a link to these legal terms in a prominent spot on your web page. Make sure you provide a mechanism for collecting users' assents to the terms.

Checklist Items:

Disclaimer on Liability of Users' Infringement of Intellectual Property Rights
Indemnity and Release
Ethics and Fraud Monitoring
Classified Ads Requirements
Age Requirements
Disclaimer of Warranties
Disclaimer of Third-Party Content
Limitation of Liability
Removal of Links
Software Download and Shareware

Submission of Ideas
Responsibility for Minors
Parental Control and Child Safety
Disclaimer Regarding Multimedia Search Results Located through Search Engines
Investment and Tax Information Disclaimer
Professional Information Disclaimer
Open Directory Disclaimer
Advertising Disclaimers
Non-Waiver and Severability
Prohibition on Resale, Assignment, or Sublicensing of Rights
Successors and Assigns
Trademark, Patent, and Copyright Notices
Arbitration, Governing Law, and Forum for Disputes

Spam Policy Module

Implement the necessary mechanism to protect your users from spam. Draft a clear policy stating your web site's position toward spam. Review the applicable laws.

Checklist Items:

Provide a definition of spam.
Provide an anti-spam policy for the site.
Inform users about spam-preventing mechanisms.

Security Module

Checklist Items:

What types of user authentication mechanisms are provided?
What types of security mechanisms are in place to prevent the loss, misuse, or alteration of information?
What information is provided to help users secure their transactions online?

Chapter 4

Web Legal Diagnosis and Report

The final step of our system of web due diligence is the web status report. This document includes a detailed description of the findings of the due-diligence process and the recommendations or actions to be adopted in order to minimize legal exposure to the web site.

Though not the same, the report may be likened to the *Reports of the Audited Financial Statements of a Corporation*. The summarized information will provide the management, shareholders, and board of directors of the web site owning firm with an overview of the weaknesses and strengths of the web site, and the corresponding recommendations to make the legal position of the web site more sound.

The results must be analyzed by the management and legal counsel in order to adopt a complete set of remedies to eliminate any weakness detected, and to prevent similar legal exposure in the future.

Information contained in this review of the legal aspects of the web site may require changes in the web site's structure, and may even result in a change of the company's corporate structure.

Recommendations included in the report must be periodically reviewed to verify their implementation. The firm may opt to assign a specific individual to supervise this implementation. This may require the collaboration of many areas within the firm.

Epilogue: The New Frontier Is Here

The legal aspects of the World Wide Web certainly are very complex. This complexity is probably the new frontier for legal professionals, and it is here. Crossing this frontier will depend not only on our capacity and skills, but also on the appropriate symbiosis of law and the technology environment.

The Internet has become woven into our everyday lives. It is apparent that there is no going back to the pre-Internet times, which were not so long ago. We have no choice, then, but to come to terms with the new technologies of the Internet, and to realize that the environment will require new legal rules, many of which we cannot even begin to imagine.

The question then is: What lies ahead? Few can say they have the answer. How will society change its policies to face the changes brought about by the technological evolution? What will be the legal responses to the many challenges that the Internet will continue to bring?

The following edited cases illustrate some of the issues courts are being asked to resolve. *Brookfield Communications v. West Coast Entertainment* considers the question of whether it is acceptable to use someone else's trademark in the domain name of one's web site and in the site's meta-tags. In

PACCAR v. TeleScan Technologies, the court grapples with a similar trademark infringement case, and prohibits a company from using another company's trademark names in its domain names, meta-tags, and web sites, and actually forces the first company to transfer registration and ownership of its domain names to the complaining company. In *Universal City Studios v. Reimerdes*, the defendant company posted code on its web site that could be used to decode encrypted digital movies by unlicensed users, and also linked its web site to many other sites where the code was available. The court found in the plaintiff company's favor. *PETA v. Doughney* deals with web site registration issues, where a web site registration interferes with a trademark name. The issues presented by these cases illustrate some of the many problems that are now beginning to emerge in the online world.

Appendix A

Brookfield Communications, Inc., Plaintiff-Appellant, v. West Coast Entertainment Corporation, Defendant-Appellee

174 F.3d 1036 (9th Circ. 1999)

Opinion: O'Scannlain, Circuit Judge

We must venture into cyberspace to determine whether federal trademark and unfair competition laws prohibit a video rental store chain from using an entertainment-industry information provider's trademark in the domain name of its web site and in its web site's meta-tags.

Part I

Brookfield Communications, Inc. ("Brookfield") appeals the district court's denial of its motion for a preliminary injunction prohibiting West Coast Entertainment Corporation ("West Coast") from using in commerce terms confusingly similar to Brookfield's trademark, "MovieBuff." Brookfield gathers and sells information about the entertainment industry. Founded in 1987 for the purpose of creating and marketing software and services for professionals in the entertainment industry, Brookfield initially offered software applications featuring information such as recent film submissions, industry credits, professional contacts, and future projects. These offerings targeted major Hollywood film studios, independent production companies, agents, actors, directors, and producers.

Brookfield expanded into the broader consumer market with computer software featuring a searchable database containing entertainment-industry related information marketed under the "MovieBuff" mark around December 1993*{all notes omitted}*. Brookfield's "MovieBuff" software now targets smaller companies and individual consumers who are not interested in purchasing Brookfield's professional-level alternative, The Studio System, and includes comprehensive, searchable, entertainment-industry databases and related software applications containing information such as movie credits, box office receipts, films in development, film release schedules, entertainment news, and listings of executives, agents, actors, and directors. This "MovieBuff" software comes in three versions—(1) the MovieBuff Pro Bundle, (2) the MovieBuff Pro, and (3) MovieBuff—and is sold through various retail stores, such as Borders, Virgin Megastores, Nobody Beats the Wiz, The Writer's Computer Store, Book City, and Samuel French Bookstores.

Sometime in 1996, Brookfield attempted to register the World Wide Web ("the Web") domain name "moviebuff.com" with Network Solutions, Inc. ("Network Solutions"), but was informed that the requested domain name had already been registered by West Coast. Brookfield subsequently registered "brookfieldcomm.com" in May 1996 and "moviebuffonline.com" in September 1996. Sometime in 1996 or 1997, Brookfield began using its web sites to sell its "MovieBuff" computer software and to offer an Internet-based searchable database marketed under the "MovieBuff" mark. Brookfield sells its "MovieBuff" computer software through its "brookfieldcomm.com" and "moviebuff-online.com" web sites and offers subscribers online access to the MovieBuff database itself at its "inhollywood.com" web site.

On August 19, 1997, Brookfield applied to the Patent and Trademark Office (PTO) for federal registration of "MovieBuff" as a mark to designate both goods and services. Its trademark application describes its product as "computer software providing data and information in the field of the motion picture and television industries." Its service mark application describes its service as "providing multiple-user access to an online network database offering data and information in the field of the motion picture and television industries." Both federal trademark registrations issued on September 29, 1998. Brookfield had previously obtained a California state trademark registration for the mark "MovieBuff" covering "computer software" in 1994.

In October 1998, Brookfield learned that West Coast—one of the nation's largest video rental store chains with over 500 stores—intended to launch a web site at "moviebuff.com" containing, *inter alia*, a searchable entertainment database similar to "MovieBuff." West Coast had registered "moviebuff.com" with Network Solutions on February 6, 1996, and claims that it chose the domain name because the term "Movie Buff" is part of its service mark, "The Movie Buff's Movie Store," on which a federal registration issued in 1991 covering "retail store services featuring video cassettes and video game cartridges" and "rental of video cassettes and video game cartridges." West Coast notes further that, since at least 1988, it has also used various phrases including the term "Movie Buff" to promote goods and services available at its video stores in Massachusetts, including "The Movie Buff's Gift Guide"; "The Movie Buff's Gift Store"; "Calling All Movie Buffs!"; "Good News Movie Buffs!"; "Movie Buffs, Show Your Stuff!"; "the Perfect Stocking Stuffer for the Movie Buff!"; "A Movie Buff's Top Ten"; "The Movie Buff Discovery Program"; "Movie Buff Picks"; "Movie Buff Series"; "Movie Buff Selection Program"; and "Movie Buff Film Series."

On November 10, Brookfield delivered to West Coast a cease-and-desist letter alleging that West Coast's planned use of the "moviebuff.com" would violate Brookfield's trademark rights; as a "courtesy" Brookfield attached a copy of a complaint that it threatened to file if West Coast did not desist.

The next day, West Coast issued a press release announcing the imminent launch of its web site full of "movie reviews, Hollywood news and gossip, provocative commentary, and coverage of the independent film scene and films in production." The press release declared that the site would feature "an extensive database, which aids consumers in making educated decisions about the rental and purchase of" movies and would also allow customers to purchase movies, accessories, and other entertainment-related merchandise on the web site.

Brookfield fired back immediately with a visit to the United States District Court for the Central District of California, and this lawsuit was born. In its first amended complaint filed on November 18, 1998, Brookfield alleged principally that West Coast's proposed offering of online services at "moviebuff.com" would constitute trademark infringement and unfair competition in violation of sections 32 and 43(a) of the Lanham Act, *15 U.S.C. §§ 1114,* 1125(a). Soon thereafter, Brookfield applied *ex parte* for a temporary restraining order (TRO) enjoining West Coast "from using . . . in any manner . . . the mark MOVIEBUFF, or any other term or terms likely to cause confusion therewith, including *moviebuff.com*, as West Coast's domain name, . . . as the name of West Coast's website service, in buried code or meta-tags on their home page or web pages, or in connection with the retrieval of data or information on other goods or services."

On November 27, West Coast filed an opposition brief in which it argued first that Brookfield could not prevent West Coast from using "moviebuff.com" in commerce because West Coast was the senior user. West Coast claimed that it was the first user of "MovieBuff" because it had used its federally registered trademark, "The Movie Buff's Movie Store," since 1986 in advertisements, promotions, and letterhead in connection with retail services featuring videocassettes and video game cartridges. Alternatively, West Coast claimed seniority on the basis that it had garnered common-law rights in the domain name by using "moviebuff.com" before Brookfield began offering its "MovieBuff" Internet-based searchable database on the Web. In addition to asserting seniority, West Coast contended that its planned use of "moviebuff.com" would not cause a likelihood of confusion with Brookfield's trademark "MovieBuff" and thus would not violate the Lanham Act.

The district court heard arguments on the TRO motion on November 30. Later that day, the district court issued an order construing Brookfield's TRO motion as a motion for a preliminary injunction and denying it. The district court concluded that West Coast was the senior user of the mark "MovieBuff" for both of the reasons asserted by West Coast. The court also determined that Brookfield had not established a likelihood of confusion.

Brookfield responded by filing a notice of appeal from the denial of preliminary injunction followed by a motion in the district court for injunction pending appeal, which motion the district court denied. On January 16, 1999, West Coast launched its web site at "moviebuff.com." Fearing that West Coast's fully operational web site would cause it irreparable injury, Brookfield filed an emergency motion for injunction pending appeal with this court a few days later. On February 24, we granted Brookfield's motion and entered an order enjoining West Coast "from using, or facilitating the use of, in any manner, including advertising and promotion, the mark MOVIEBUFF, or any other term or terms likely to cause confusion therewith, including *@moviebuff.com* or *movie-*

buff.com, as the name of West Coast's web site service, in buried code or metatags on its home page or web pages, or in connection with the retrieval of data or information on other goods or services." The injunction was to take effect upon the posting of a $25,000 bond in the district court by Brookfield. We scheduled oral argument on an expedited basis for March 10.

West Coast thereupon filed a motion for reconsideration and modification—seeking a stay of the injunction pending appeal and an increase in the bond requirement to $400,000—which we denied. After oral argument on March 10, we ordered that our previously issued injunction remain in effect pending the issuance of this opinion.

Part II

To resolve the legal issues before us, we must first understand the basics of the Internet and the World Wide Web. Because we will be delving into technical corners of the Internet—dealing with features such as domain names and metatags—we explain in some detail what all these things are and provide a general overview of the relevant technology.

The Internet is a global network of interconnected computers which allows individuals and organizations around the world to communicate and to share information with one another. The Web, a collection of information resources contained in documents located on individual computers around the world, is the most widely used and fastest-growing part of the Internet except perhaps for electronic mail ("e-mail"). *{Most references omitted}*. With the Web becoming an important mechanism for commerce, companies are racing to stake out their place in cyberspace. Prevalent on the Web are multimedia "web pages"—computer data files written in Hypertext Markup Language (HTML)—which contain information such as text, pictures, sounds, audio and video recordings, and links to other web pages.

Each web page has a corresponding domain address, which is an identifier somewhat analogous to a telephone number or street address. Domain names consist of a second-level domain—simply a term or series of terms (e.g., westcoastvideo)—followed by a top-level domain, many of which describe the nature of the enterprise. Top-level domains include ".com" (commercial), ".edu" (educational), ".org" (non-profit and miscellaneous organizations), ".gov" (government), ".net" (networking provider), and ".mil" (military). Commercial entities generally use the ".com" top-level domain, which also serves as a catchall top-level domain. *See id.* To obtain a domain name, an individual or entity files an application with Network Solutions listing the domain name the applicant wants. Because each web page must have an unique domain name, Network Solutions checks to see whether the requested domain name has already been assigned to someone else. If so, the applicant must choose a different domain name. Other than requiring an applicant to make certain representations, Network Solutions does not make an independent determination about a registrant's right to use a particular domain name.

Using a web browser, such as Netscape Navigator or Microsoft Internet Explorer, a cyber "surfer" may navigate the Web—searching for, communicating with, and retrieving information from various web sites. A specific web site is most easily located by using its domain name. Upon entering a domain name into the web browser, the corresponding web site will quickly appear on the computer screen. Sometimes, however, a Web surfer will not know the domain name of the site he is looking for, whereupon he has two principal options: trying to guess the domain name or seeking the assistance of an Internet "search engine."

Oftentimes, an Internet user will begin by hazarding a guess at the domain name, especially if there is an obvious domain name to try. Web users often assume, as a rule of thumb, that the domain name of a particular company will be the company name followed by ".com." For example, one looking for Kraft Foods, Inc. might try "kraftfoods.com," and indeed this web site contains information on Kraft's many food products. Sometimes, a trademark is better known than the company itself, in which case a web surfer may assume that the domain address will be "'trademark'.com." One interested in today's news would do well visiting "usatoday.com," which features, as one would expect, breaking stories from Gannett's *USA Today*. Guessing domain names, however, is not a risk-free activity. The web surfer who assumes that "'X'.com" will always correspond to the web site of company X or trademark X will, however, sometimes be misled. One looking for the latest information on Panavision, International, L.P., would sensibly try "panavision.com." Until recently, that web surfer would have instead found a web site owned by Dennis Toeppen featuring photographs of the City of Pana, Illinois. Having registered several domain names that logically would have corresponded to the web sites of major companies such as Panavision, Delta Airlines, Neiman Marcus, Lufthansa, Toeppen sought to sell "panavision.com" to Panavision, which gives one a taste of some of the trademark issues that have arisen in cyberspace.

A web surfer's second option when he does not know the domain name is to utilize an Internet search engine, such as Yahoo, Altavista, or Lycos. When a keyword is entered, the search engine processes it through a self-created index of web sites to generate a (sometimes long) list relating to the entered keyword. Each search engine uses its own algorithm to arrange indexed materials in sequence, so the list of web sites that any particular set of keywords will bring up may differ depending on the search engine used. Search engines look for keywords in places such as domain names, actual text on the web page, and meta-tags. Meta-tags are HTML code intended to describe the contents of the web site. There are different types of meta-tags, but those of principal concern to us are the "description" and "keyword" meta-tags. The description meta-tags are intended to describe the web site; the keyword meta-tags, at least in theory, contain keywords relating to the contents of the web site. The more often a term appears in the meta-tags and in the text of the web page, the more likely it is that the web page will be "hit" in a search for that keyword and the higher on the list of "hits" the web page will appear.

With this basic understanding of the Internet and the Web, we may now analyze the legal issues before us.

Part III

We review the district court's denial of preliminary injunctive relief for an abuse of discretion. Under this standard, reversal is appropriate only if the district court based its decision on clearly erroneous findings of fact or erroneous legal principles. "A plaintiff is entitled to a preliminary injunction in a trademark case when he demonstrates either (1) a combination of probable success on the merits and the possibility of irreparable injury or (2) the existence of serious questions going to the merits and that the balance of hardships tips sharply in his favor." *Sardi's Restaurant Corp. v. Sardie, 755 F.2d 719, 723 (9th Cir. 1985).* To establish a trademark infringement claim under section 32 of the Lanham Act or an unfair competition claim under section 43(a) of the Lanham Act, Brookfield must establish that West Coast is using a mark confusingly similar to a valid, protectable trademark of Brookfield's. The district court denied Brookfield's motion for preliminary injunctive relief because it concluded that Brookfield had failed to establish that it was the senior user of the "MovieBuff" mark or that West Coast's use of the "moviebuff.com" domain name created a likelihood of confusion.

We review each of the district court's conclusions in turn.

Part IV

To resolve whether West Coast's use of "moviebuff.com" constitutes trademark infringement or unfair competition, we must first determine whether Brookfield has a valid, protectable trademark interest in the "MovieBuff" mark. Brookfield's registration of the mark on the Principal Register in the Patent and Trademark Office constitutes prima facie evidence of the validity of the registered mark and of Brookfield's exclusive right to use the mark on the goods and services specified in the registration. Nevertheless, West Coast can rebut this presumption by showing that it used the mark in commerce first, since a fundamental tenet of trademark law is that ownership of an inherently distinctive mark such as "MovieBuff" is governed by priority of use. The first to use a mark is deemed the "senior" user and has the right to enjoin "junior" users from using confusingly similar marks in the same industry and market or within the senior user's natural zone of expansion.

It is uncontested that Brookfield began selling "MovieBuff" software in 1993 and that West Coast did not use "moviebuff.com" until 1996. According to West Coast, however, the fact that it has used "The Movie Buff's Movie Store" as a trademark since 1986 makes it the first user for purposes of trademark priority. In the alternative, West Coast claims priority on the basis that it used "moviebuff.com" in commerce before Brookfield began offering its "Movie-Buff" searchable database on the Internet. We analyze these contentions in turn.

A

Conceding that the first time that it *actually* used "moviebuff.com" was in 1996, West Coast argues that its earlier use of "The Movie Buff's Movie Store" constitutes use of "moviebuff.com." West Coast has not provided any Ninth Circuit precedent approving of this constructive use theory, but neither has Brookfield pointed us to any case law rejecting it. We are not without guidance, however, as our sister circuits have explicitly recognized the ability of a trademark owner to claim priority in a mark based on the first use date of a similar, but technically distinct, mark—but only in the exceptionally narrow instance where "the previously used mark is 'the legal equivalent of the mark in question or indistinguishable therefrom' such that consumers 'consider both as the same mark.'" *Data Concepts, Inc. v. Digital Consulting, Inc., 150 F.3d 620, 623 (6th Cir. 1998).*

This constructive use theory is known as "tacking," as the trademark holder essentially seeks to "tack" his first use date in the earlier mark onto the subsequent mark.

We agree that tacking should be allowed if two marks are so similar that consumers generally would regard them as essentially the same. Where such is the case, the new mark serves the same identificatory function as the old mark. Giving the trademark owner the same rights in the new mark as he has in the old helps to protect source-identifying trademarks from appropriation by competitors and thus furthers the trademark law's objective of reducing the costs that customers incur in shopping and making purchasing decisions.

Without tacking, a trademark owner's priority in his mark would be reduced each time he made the slightest alteration to the mark, which would discourage him from altering the mark in response to changing consumer preferences, evolving aesthetic developments, or new advertising and marketing styles. In *Hess's of Allentown, Inc. v. National Bellas Hess, Inc.*, for example, a department store ("Allentown") with trademark rights in the terms "Hess Brothers" and "Hess" dating from 1899 began promoting itself in 1952 instead as "Hess's," largely because customers and employees commonly referred to the store as "Hess's" rather than "Hess Brothers" or "Hess." Another department store ("Bellas") first used "Hess" in its mark around 1932. In light of the fact that Allentown first used "Hess's" after Bellas commenced using "Hess," Bellas would have priority on the basis of the actual first use dates of those two marks. Even though Allentown had acquired over a half-century's worth of goodwill in the essentially identical marks "Hess" and "Hess Brothers," Allentown no longer had trademark rights in those terms because it had ceased using those marks when it adopted "Hess's." Nevertheless, the Trademark Board allowed the owner of "Hess's" to tack his first use date of "Hess Brothers" and "Hess" onto "Hess's" since those terms were viewed as identical by the public.

The standard for "tacking," however, is exceedingly strict: "The marks must create the *same, continuing commercial impression*, and the later mark should not materially differ from or alter the character of the mark attempted to be tacked." *Van Dyne-Crotty, 926 F.2d at 1159.* In other words, "the previously used mark must be the *legal equivalent* of the mark in question or indistinguishable therefrom, and the consumer should consider both as the same mark." *Id.* This standard is considerably higher than the standard for "likelihood of confusion," which we discuss *infra*.

The Federal Circuit, for example, concluded that priority in "CLOTHES THAT WORK. FOR THE WORK YOU DO" could not be tacked onto "CLOTHES THAT WORK." *See Van Dyne-Crotty, 926 F.2d at 1160* (holding that the shorter phrase was *not* the legal equivalent of the longer mark). The Sixth Circuit held that "DCI" and "dci" were too dissimilar to support tacking. *See Data Concepts, 150 F.3d at 623-24.* And the Trademark Board has rejected tacking in a case involving "American Mobilphone" with a star and stripe design and "American Mobilphone Paging" with the identical design, *see American Paging, Inc. v. American Mobilphone, Inc., 13 U.S.P.Q.2D (BNA) 2036 (T.T. A.B. 1989).*

In contrast to cases such as *Van Dyne-Crotty* and *American Paging*, which were close questions, the present case is clear cut: "The Movie Buff's Movie Store" and "moviebuff.com" are very different, in that the latter contains three fewer words, drops the possessive, omits a space, and adds ".com" to the end. Because West Coast failed to make the slightest showing that consumers view these terms as identical, we must conclude that West Coast cannot tack its priority in "The Movie Buff's Movie Store" onto "moviebuff.com." As the Federal Circuit explained, "[I]t would be clearly contrary to well-established principles of trademark law to sanction the tacking of a mark with a narrow commercial impression onto one with a broader commercial impression." *Van Dyne-Crotty, 926 F.2d at 1160* (noting that prior use of "SHAPE UP" could not be tacked onto "EGO," that prior use of "ALTER EGO" could not be tacked onto "EGO," and that prior use of "Marco Polo" could not be tacked onto "Polo").

Since tacking does not apply, we must therefore conclude that Brookfield is the senior user because it marketed "MovieBuff" products well before West Coast began using "moviebuff.com" in commerce: West Coast's use of "The Movie Buff's Movie Store" is simply irrelevant. Our priority determination is consistent with the decisions of our sister circuits in *Lone Star Steakhouse & Saloon, Inc. v. Longhorn Steaks, Inc., 106 F.3d 355, 362-63 (11th Cir. 1997), modified by, 122 F.3d 1379 (11th Cir. 1997)* (per curiam), and *J. Wiss & Sons Co. v. W. E. Bassett Co., 59 C.C.P.A. 1269, 462 F.2d 567, 568-69 (C.C.P.A. 1972).* Like the present case, *J. Wiss & Sons* is a three-competing-trademark situation in which one company owned a single mark with a first use date in between the first use dates of the two marks owned by the other company. In that case, the intervening mark ("Trim") was found to be confusingly similar with the later mark ("Trim-Line"), but not with the earlier mark ("Quick-Trim"); similarly here, the intervening mark ("MovieBuff") is purported to be confusingly similar with the later mark "moviebuff.com," *see infra* Part V, but is not confusingly similar with the earlier used mark "The Movie Buff's Movie Store." The Court of Customs and Patent Appeals (now the Court of Appeals for the Federal Circuit) concluded that priority depended upon which of the two confusingly similar marks was used first—disregarding the first use date of the

earlier-used mark since it was not confusingly similar with the others. It thus awarded priority to the holder of the intervening mark, as we do similarly here.

Longhorn Steaks, involving the same basic three-competing-trademark situation, is particularly instructive. The defendant owned the mark "Lone Star Steaks" with a first use date between the plaintiff's earlier used mark "Lone Star Cafe" and its later used mark "Lone Star Steakhouse & Saloon." In its initial opinion, the Eleventh Circuit awarded priority to the holder of "Lone Star Steaks" on the basis that "Lone Star Steaks" was used before "Lone Star Steakhouse & Saloon." The Eleventh Circuit, however, later modified its opinion, stating that the conclusion reached in its initial opinion would be correct only if defendant's "Lone Star Steaks" was not confusingly similar to plaintiff's earlier used mark, "Lone Star Cafe."

West Coast makes a half-hearted claim that "MovieBuff" is confusingly similar to its earlier used mark "The Movie Buff's Movie Store." If this were so, West Coast would undoubtedly be the senior user. "Of course, if the symbol or device is already in general use, employed in such a manner that its adoption as an index of source or origin would only produce confusion and mislead the public, it is not susceptible of adoption as a trademark." *Hanover Star Milling Co. v. Metcalf, 240 U.S. 403, 415, 60 L. Ed. 713, 36 S. Ct. 357 (1916).* West Coast, however, essentially conceded that "MovieBuff" and "The Movie Buff's Movie Store" are not confusingly similar when it stated in its pre-argument papers that it does not allege actual confusion between "MovieBuff" and West Coast's federally registered mark. We cannot think of more persuasive evidence that there is no *likelihood* of confusion between these two marks than the fact that they have been simultaneously used for five years without causing any consumers to be confused as to who makes what. The failure to *prove* instances of actual confusion is *not* dispositive against a trademark plaintiff, because actual confusion is hard to prove; difficulties in gathering evidence of actual confusion make its absence generally unnoteworthy. West Coast, however, did not state that it could not *prove* actual confusion; rather, it conceded that there has been none. This is a crucial difference. Although there may be the rare case in which a likelihood of future confusion is possible even where it is conceded that two marks have been used simultaneously for years with no resulting confusion, West Coast has not shown this to be such a case.

Our conclusion comports with the position of the PTO, which effectively announced its finding of no likelihood of confusion between "The Movie Buff's Movie Store" and "MovieBuff" when it placed the latter on the principal register despite West Coast's prior registration of "The Movie Buff's Movie Store." Priority is accordingly to be determined on the basis of whether Brookfield used "MovieBuff" or West Coast used "moviebuff.com" first.

B

West Coast argues that we are mixing apples and oranges when we compare its first use date of "moviebuff.com" with the first sale date of "MovieBuff" software. West Coast reminds us that Brookfield uses the "MovieBuff" mark with both computer software and the provision of an Internet database; accord-

ing to West Coast, its use of "moviebuff.com" can cause confusion only with respect to the latter. West Coast asserts that we should accordingly determine seniority by comparing West Coast's first use date of "moviebuff.com" not with when Brookfield first sold software, but with when it first offered its database online.

As an initial matter, we note that West Coast's argument is premised on the assumption that its use of "moviebuff.com" does not cause confusion between its web site and Brookfield's "MovieBuff" software products. Even though Brookfield's computer software and West Coast's offerings on its web site are not identical products, likelihood of confusion can still result where, for example, there is a likelihood of expansion in product lines. As the leading trademark commentator explains: "When a senior user of a mark on product line A expands later into product line B and finds an intervening user, priority in product line B is determined by whether the expansion is 'natural' in that customers would have been confused as to source or affiliation at the time of the intervening user's appearance." *2 McCarthy § 16:5.* We need not, however, decide whether the Web was within Brookfield's natural zone of expansion, because we conclude that Brookfield's use of "MovieBuff" as a service mark preceded West Coast's use.

Brookfield first used "MovieBuff" on its Internet-based products and services in August 1997, so West Coast can prevail only if it establishes first use earlier than that. In the literal sense of the word, West Coast "used" the term "moviebuff.com" when it registered that domain address in February 1996. Registration with Network Solutions, however, does not in itself constitute "use" for purposes of acquiring trademark priority. The Lanham Act grants trademark protection only to marks that are used to identify and to distinguish goods or services in commerce—which typically occurs when a mark is used in conjunction with the actual sale of goods or services. The purpose of a trademark is to help consumers identify the source, but a mark cannot serve a source-identifying function if the public has never seen the mark and thus is not meritorious of trademark protection until it is used in public in a manner that creates an association among consumers between the mark and the mark's owner.

Such use requirement is firmly established in the case law, and, moreover, is embodied in the Lanham Act itself. In fact, Congress amended the Lanham Act in 1988 to strengthen this "use in commerce" requirement, making clear that trademark rights can be conveyed only through "the bona fide use of a mark in the ordinary course of trade, and not [use] made merely to reserve a mark." *15 U.S.C. § 1127.* Congress provided more specifically:

For purposes of this chapter, a mark shall be deemed to be in use in commerce—

(1) on goods when—

(A) it is placed in any manner on the goods or their containers or the displays associated therewith or on the tags or labels affixed thereto, or if the nature of the goods makes such placement impracticable, then on documents associated with the goods or their sale, and

(B) the goods are sold or transported in commerce, and

(2) on services when it is used or displayed in the sale or advertising of services and the services are rendered in commerce, or the services are rendered in more than one state or in the United States and a foreign country and the person rendering the services is engaged in commerce in connection with the services. *Id.*

The district court, while recognizing that mere registration of a domain name was not sufficient to constitute commercial use for purposes of the Lanham Act, nevertheless held that registration of a domain name with the intent to use it commercially was sufficient to convey trademark rights. This analysis, however, contradicts both the express statutory language and the case law which firmly establishes that trademark rights are not conveyed through mere intent to use a mark commercially, nor through mere preparation to use a term as a trademark.

West Coast no longer disputes that its use—for purposes of the Lanham Act—of "moviebuff.com" did not commence until after February 1996. It instead relies on the alternate argument that its rights vested when it began using "moviebuff.com" in e-mail correspondence with lawyers and customers sometime in mid-1996. West Coast's argument is not without support in our case law—we have indeed held that trademark rights can vest even before any goods or services are actually sold if "the totality of [one's] prior actions, taken together, [can] establish a right to use the trademark." *New West, 595 F.2d at 1200.* Under *New West*, however, West Coast must establish that its e-mail correspondence constituted "use in a way sufficiently public to identify or distinguish the marked goods in an appropriate segment of the public mind as those of the adopter of the mark.'' *Id.*

West Coast fails to meet this standard. Its purported "use" is akin to putting one's mark "on a business office door sign, letterheads, architectural drawings, etc." or on a prototype displayed to a potential buyer, both of which have been held to be insufficient to establish trademark rights. Although widespread publicity of a company's mark, such as Marvel Comics' announcement to 13 million comic book readers that "Plasma" would be the title of a new comic book, or the mailing of 430,000 solicitation letters with one's mark to potential subscribers of a magazine, may be sufficient to create an association among the public between the mark and West Coast, mere use in limited e-mail correspondence with lawyers and a few customers is not.

West Coast first announced its web site at "moviebuff.com" in a public and widespread manner in a press release of November 11, 1998, and thus it is not until at least that date that it first used the "moviebuff.com" mark for purposes of the Lanham Act. Accordingly, West Coast's argument that it has seniority because it used "moviebuff.com" before Brookfield used "MovieBuff" as a service mark fails on its own terms. West Coast's first use date was *neither* February 1996 when it registered its domain name with Network Solutions as the district court had concluded, *nor* April 1996 when it first used "moviebuff.com" in e-mail communications, but *rather* November 1998 when it first made a widespread and public announcement about the imminent launch of its web site. Thus, West Coast's first use of "moviebuff.com" was preceded by Brookfield's first use of "MovieBuff" in conjunction with its online database, making Brookfield the senior user.

For the foregoing reasons, we conclude that the district court erred in concluding that Brookfield failed to establish a likelihood of success on its claim of being the senior user.

Part V

Establishing seniority, however, is only half the battle. Brookfield must also show that the public is likely to be somehow confused about the source or sponsorship of West Coast's "moviebuff.com" web site—and somehow to associate that site with Brookfield. The Supreme Court has described "the basic objectives of trademark law" as follows: "[T]rademark law, by preventing others from copying a source-identifying mark, 'reduces the customer's costs of shopping and making purchasing decisions,' for it quickly and easily assures a potential customer that this item—the item with this mark—is made by the same producer as other similarly marked items that he or she liked (or disliked) in the past. At the same time, the law helps assure a producer that it (and not an imitating competitor) will reap the financial, reputation-related rewards associated with a desirable product." *Qualitex, 514 U.S. at 163-64* (internal citations omitted). Where two companies each use a different mark and the simultaneous use of those marks does not cause the consuming public to be confused as to who makes what, granting one company exclusive rights over both marks does nothing to further the objectives of the trademark laws; in fact, prohibiting the use of a mark that the public has come to associate with a company would actually contravene the intended purposes of the trademark law by making it *more* difficult to identify and to distinguish between different brands of goods.

"The core element of trademark infringement is the likelihood of confusion, i.e., whether the similarity of the marks is likely to confuse customers about the source of the products." *Official Airline Guides, 6 F.3d at 1391.* We look to the following factors for guidance in determining the likelihood of confusion: similarity of the conflicting designations; relatedness or proximity of the two companies' products or services; strength of Brookfield's mark; marketing channels used; degree of care likely to be exercised by purchasers in selecting goods; West Coast's intent in selecting its mark; evidence of actual confusion; and likelihood of expansion in product lines. These eight factors are often referred to as the *Sleekcraft* factors.

A word of caution: this eight-factor test for likelihood of confusion is pliant. Some factors are much more important than others, and the relative importance of each individual factor will be case-specific. Although some factors—such as the similarity of the marks and whether the two companies are direct competitors—will always be important, it is often possible to reach a conclusion with respect to likelihood of confusion after considering only a subset of the factors. Moreover, the foregoing list does not purport to be exhaustive, and non-listed variables may often be quite important. We must be acutely aware of excessive rigidity when applying the law in the Internet context; emerging technologies require a flexible approach.

A

We begin by comparing the allegedly infringing mark to the federally registered mark. The similarity of the marks will always be an important factor. Where the two marks are entirely dissimilar, there is no likelihood of confusion. "Pepsi" does not infringe Coca-Cola's "Coke." Nothing further need be said. Even where there is precise identity of a complainant's and an alleged infringer's mark, there may be no consumer confusion—and thus no trademark infringement—if the alleged infringer is in a different geographic area or in a wholly different industry. Nevertheless, the more similar the marks in terms of appearance, sound, and meaning, the greater the likelihood of confusion. In analyzing this factor, "the marks must be considered in their entirety and as they appear in the market-place," *Goss, 6 F.3d at 1392,* with similarities weighed more heavily than differences.

In the present case, the district court found West Coast's domain name "moviebuff.com" to be quite different than Brookfield's domain name "moviebuffonline.com." Comparison of domain names, however, is irrelevant as a matter of law, since the Lanham Act requires that the allegedly infringing mark be compared with the claimant's *trademark*, which here is "MovieBuff," not "moviebuffonline.com." Properly framed, it is readily apparent that West Coast's allegedly infringing mark is essentially identical to Brookfield's mark "MovieBuff." In terms of appearance, there are differences in capitalization and the addition of ".com" in West Coast's complete domain name, but these differences are inconsequential in light of the fact that web addresses are not caps-sensitive and that the ".com" top-level domain signifies the site's commercial nature.

Looks aren't everything, so we consider the similarity of sound and meaning. The two marks are pronounced the same way, except that one would say "dot com" at the end of West Coast's mark. Because many companies use domain names comprised of ".com" as the top-level domain with their corporate name or trademark as the second-level domain, the addition of ".com" is of diminished importance in distinguishing the mark. The irrelevance of the ".com" becomes further apparent once we consider similarity in meaning. The domain name is more than a mere address: like trademarks, second-level domain names communicate information as to source. As we explained in Part II, many Web users are likely to associate "moviebuff.com" with the trademark "MovieBuff," thinking that it is operated by the company that makes "MovieBuff" products and services. Courts, in fact, have routinely concluded that marks were essentially identical in similar contexts. As "MovieBuff" and "moviebuff.com" are, for all intents and purposes, identical in terms of sight, sound, and meaning, we conclude that the similarity factor weighs heavily in favor of Brookfield.

The similarity of marks alone, as we have explained, does not necessarily lead to consumer confusion. Accordingly, we must proceed to consider the relatedness of the products and services offered. Related goods are generally more likely than unrelated goods to confuse the public as to the producers of the goods. In light of the virtual identity of marks, if they were used with identical products or services likelihood of confusion would follow as a matter of course. If, on the other hand, Brookfield and West Coast did not compete to any extent whatsoever, the likelihood of confusion would probably be remote. A Web surfer who accessed "moviebuff.com" and reached a web site advertising the services of Schlumberger Ltd. (a large oil drilling company) would be unlikely to think that Brookfield had entered the oil drilling business or was sponsoring the oil driller. At the least, Brookfield would bear the heavy burden of demonstrating (through other relevant factors) that consumers were likely to be confused as to source or affiliation in such a circumstance.

The district court classified West Coast and Brookfield as non-competitors largely on the basis that Brookfield is primarily an information provider while West Coast primarily rents and sells videotapes. It noted that West Coast's web site is used more by the somewhat curious video consumer who wants general movie information, while entertainment industry professionals, aspiring entertainment executives and professionals, and highly focused moviegoers are more likely to need or to want the more detailed information provided by "MovieBuff." This analysis, however, overemphasizes differences in principal lines of business, as we have previously instructed that "the relatedness of each company's prime directive isn't relevant." *Dreamwerks, 142 F.3d at 1131.* Instead, the focus is on whether the consuming public is likely somehow to associate West Coast's products with Brookfield. *See id.* Here, both companies offer products and services relating to the entertainment industry generally, and their principal lines of business both relate to movies specifically and are not as different as guns and toys, or computer circuit boards and the *Rocky Horror Picture Show.* Thus, Brookfield and West Coast are not properly characterized as non-competitors.

Not only are they not non-competitors, the competitive proximity of their products is actually quite high. Just as Brookfield's "MovieBuff" is a searchable database with detailed information on films, West Coast's web site features a similar searchable database, which Brookfield points out is licensed from a direct competitor of Brookfield. Undeniably then, the products are used for similar purposes. "The rights of the owner of a registered trademark . . . extend to any goods related in the minds of consumers," *E. Remy Martin & Co. v. Shaw-Ross Int'l Imports, Inc., 756 F.2d 1525, 1530 (11th Cir. 1985),* and Brookfield's and West Coast's products are certainly so related to some extent. The relatedness is further evidenced by the fact that the two companies compete for the patronage of an overlapping audience. The use of similar marks to offer similar products accordingly weighs heavily in favor of likelihood of confusion.

In addition to the relatedness of products, West Coast and Brookfield both utilize the Web as a marketing and advertising facility, a factor that courts have consistently recognized as exacerbating the likelihood of confusion. Both companies, apparently recognizing the rapidly growing importance of web commerce, are maneuvering to attract customers via the web. Not only do they compete for the patronage of an overlapping audience on the web, both

"MovieBuff" and "moviebuff.com" are utilized in conjunction with web-based products.

Given the virtual identity of "moviebuff.com" and "MovieBuff," the relatedness of the products and services accompanied by those marks, and the companies' simultaneous use of the Web as a marketing and advertising tool, many forms of consumer confusion are likely to result. People surfing the Web for information on "MovieBuff" may confuse "MovieBuff" with the searchable entertainment database at "moviebuff.com" and simply assume that they have reached Brookfield's web site. In the Internet context, in particular, entering a web site takes little effort—usually one click from a linked site or a search engine's list; thus, web surfers are more likely to be confused as to the ownership of a web site than traditional patrons of a brick-and-mortar store would be of a store's ownership. Alternatively, they may incorrectly believe that West Coast licensed "MovieBuff" from Brookfield, or that Brookfield otherwise sponsored West Coast's database. Other consumers may simply believe that West Coast bought out Brookfield or that they are related companies.

Yet other forms of confusion are likely to ensue. Consumers may wrongly assume that the "MovieBuff" database they were searching for is no longer offered, having been replaced by West Coast's entertainment database, and thus simply use the services at West Coast's web site. And even where people realize, immediately upon accessing "moviebuff.com," that they have reached a site operated by West Coast and wholly unrelated to Brookfield, West Coast will still have gained a customer by appropriating the goodwill that Brookfield has developed in its "MovieBuff" mark. A consumer who was originally looking for Brookfield's products or services may be perfectly content with West Coast's database (especially as it is offered free of charge); but he reached West Coast's site because of its use of Brookfield's mark as its second-level domain name, which is a misappropriation of Brookfield's goodwill by West Coast.

The district court apparently assumed that likelihood of confusion exists only when consumers are confused as to the source of a product they actually purchase. It is, however, well established that the Lanham Act protects against the many other forms of confusion that we have outlined.

The factors that we have considered so far—the similarity of marks, the relatedness of product offerings, and the overlap in marketing and advertising channels—lead us to the tentative conclusion that Brookfield has made a strong showing of likelihood of confusion. Because it is possible that the remaining factors will tip the scale back the other way if they weigh strongly enough in West Coast's favor, we consider the remaining likelihood of confusion factors, beginning with the strength of Brookfield's mark. The stronger a mark—meaning the more likely it is to be remembered and associated in the public mind with the mark's owner—the greater the protection it is accorded by the trademark laws. Marks can be conceptually classified along a spectrum of generally increasing inherent distinctiveness as generic, descriptive, suggestive, arbitrary, or fanciful. West Coast asserts that Brookfield's mark is "not terribly distinctive," by which it apparently means suggestive, but only weakly so.

KCK COMM. COLLEGE LIBRARY
7250 State Ave.
Kansas City, Kansas 66112

Although Brookfield does not seriously dispute that its mark is only suggestive, it does defend its (mark's) muscularity.

We have recognized that, unlike arbitrary or fanciful marks which are typically strong, suggestive marks are presumptively weak. As the district court recognized, placement within the conceptual distinctiveness spectrum is not the only determinant of a mark's strength, as advertising expenditures can transform a suggestive mark into a strong mark, where, for example, that mark has achieved actual marketplace recognition. Brookfield, however, has not come forth with substantial evidence establishing the widespread recognition of its mark; although it argues that its strength is established from its use of "MovieBuff" for over five years, its federal and California state registrations, and its expenditure of $100,000 in advertising its mark, the district court did not clearly err in classifying "MovieBuff" as weak. Some weak marks are weaker than others, and although "MovieBuff" falls within the weak side of the strength spectrum, the mark is not so flabby as to compel a finding of no likelihood of confusion in light of the other factors that we have considered. Importantly, Brookfield's trademark is not descriptive because it does not describe either the software product or its purpose. Instead, it is suggestive—and thus strong enough to warrant trademark protection—because it requires a mental leap from the mark to the product. Because the products involved are closely related and West Coast's domain name is nearly identical to Brookfield's trademark, the strength of the mark is of diminished importance in the likelihood of confusion analysis.

We thus turn to intent. "The law has long been established that if an infringer 'adopts his designation with the intent of deriving benefit from the reputation of the trademark or trade name, its intent may be sufficient to justify the inference that there are confusing similarities.'" *Pacific Telesis v. International Telesis Comms., 994 F.2d 1364, 1369 (9th Cir. 1993).* An inference of confusion has similarly been deemed appropriate where a mark is adopted with the intent to deceive the public. The district court found that the intent factor favored West Coast because it did not adopt the "moviebuff.com" mark with the specific purpose of infringing Brookfield's trademark. The intent prong, however, is not so narrowly confined.

This factor favors the plaintiff where the alleged infringer adopted his mark with knowledge, actual or constructive, that it was another's trademark. In the Internet context, in particular, courts have appropriately recognized that the intentional registration of a domain name knowing that the second-level domain is another company's valuable trademark weighs in favor of likelihood of confusion. There is, however, no evidence in the record that West Coast registered "moviebuff.com" with the principal intent of confusing consumers. Brookfield correctly points out that, by the time West Coast launched its web site, it *did* know of Brookfield's claim to rights in the trademark "MovieBuff." But when it registered the domain name with Network Solutions, West Coast did not know of Brookfield's rights in "MovieBuff" (at least Brookfield has not established that it did). Although Brookfield asserts that West Coast could easily have launched its web site at its alternate domain address, "westcoastvideo.com," thereby avoiding the infringement problem, West Coast claims that it had already invested considerable sums in developing its "moviebuff.com" web site by the time that Brookfield informed it of its rights in the trademark. Considered as a whole, this factor appears indeterminate.

Importantly, an intent to confuse consumers is not required for a finding of trademark infringement. Instead, this factor is only relevant to the extent that it bears upon the likelihood that consumers will be confused by the alleged infringer's mark (or to the extent that a court wishes to consider it as an equitable consideration). Here, West Coast's intent does not appear to bear upon the likelihood of confusion because it did not act with such an intent from which it is appropriate to infer consumer confusion.

The final three *Sleekcraft* factors—evidence of actual confusion, likelihood of expansion in product lines, and purchaser care—do not affect our ultimate conclusion regarding the likelihood of confusion. The first two factors do not merit extensive comment. Actual confusion is not relevant because Brookfield filed suit before West Coast began actively using the "moviebuff.com" mark and thus never had the opportunity to collect information on actual confusion. The likelihood of expansion in product lines factor is relatively unimportant where two companies already compete to a significant extent. In any case, it is neither exceedingly likely nor unlikely that West Coast will enter more directly into Brookfield's principal market, or vice versa.

Although the district court did not discuss the degree of care likely to be exercised by purchasers of the products in question, we think that this issue deserves some consideration. Likelihood of confusion is determined on the basis of a "reasonably prudent consumer." *Dreamwerks, 142 F.3d.* What is expected of this reasonably prudent consumer depends on the circumstances. We expect him to be more discerning—and less easily confused—when he is purchasing expensive items, and when the products being sold are marketed primarily to expert buyers. We recognize, however, that confusion may often be likely even in the case of expensive goods sold to discerning customers. On the other hand, when dealing with inexpensive products, customers are likely to exercise less care, thus making confusion more likely.

The complexity in this case arises because we must consider both entertainment professionals, who probably will take the time and effort to find the specific product they want, and movie devotees, who will be more easily confused as to the source of the database offered at West Coast's web site. In addition, West Coast's site is likely to be visited by many casual movie watchers. The entertainment professional, movie devotee, and casual watcher are likely to exercise high, little, and very little care, respectively. Who is the reasonably prudent consumer? Although we have not addressed the issue of purchaser care in mixed buyer classes, another circuit has held that "the standard of care to be exercised by the reasonably prudent purchaser will be equal to that of the least sophisticated consumer." *Ford Motor Co. v. Summit Motor Prods., Inc., 930 F.2d 277, 283 (3d Cir. 1991).* This is not the only approach available to us, as we could alternatively use a weighted average of the different levels of purchaser care in determining how the reasonably prudent consumer would act.

We need not, however, decide this question now because the purchaser confusion factor, even considered in the light most favorable to West Coast, is not sufficient to overcome the likelihood of confusion strongly established by the other factors we have analyzed.

West Coast makes one last ditch argument—that, even if there is a likelihood of confusion, Brookfield should be estopped from asserting its trademark rights because it waited too long to file suit. Although we have applied laches to bar trademark infringement claims, we have done so only where the trademark holder knowingly allowed the infringing mark to be used without objection for a lengthy period of time. In *E-Systems*, for example, we estopped a claimant who did not file suit until after the allegedly infringing mark had been used for eight years where the claimant had known of the infringing use for at least six years. We specifically cautioned, however, that "had defendant's encroachment been minimal, or its growth slow and steady, there would be no laches." *E-Systems, 720 F.2d at 607.* Here, although Brookfield waited over two years before notifying West Coast that its intended use of "moviebuff.com" would infringe on Brookfield's trademark, West Coast did not do anything with its domain address during that time, and Brookfield filed suit the very day that West Coast publicly announced its intention to launch a web site at "moviebuff.com." Accordingly, we conclude that Brookfield's delay was not such that it should be estopped from pursuing an otherwise meritorious claim.

In light of the foregoing analysis, we conclude that Brookfield has demonstrated a likelihood of success on its claim that West Coast's use of "moviebuff.com" violates the Lanham Act. We are fully aware that although the question of "whether confusion is likely is a factual determination woven into the law," we nevertheless must review only for clear error the district court's conclusion that the evidence of likelihood of confusion in this case was slim. Here, however, we are "left with the definite and firm conviction that a mistake has been made." *Pacific Telesis Group v. International Telesis Comms., 994 F.2d 1364, 1367 (9th Cir. 1993).*

B

So far we have considered only West Coast's use of the domain name "moviebuff.com." Because Brookfield requested that we also preliminarily enjoin West Coast from using marks confusingly similar to "MovieBuff" in meta-tags and buried code, we must also decide whether West Coast can, consistently with the trademark and unfair competition laws, use "MovieBuff" or "moviebuff.com" in its HTML code.

At first glance, our resolution of the infringement issues in the domain name context would appear to dictate a similar conclusion of likelihood of confusion with respect to West Coast's use of "moviebuff.com" in its meta-tags. Indeed, all eight likelihood of confusion factors outlined in Part V-A—with the possible exception of purchaser care, which we discuss below—apply here as they did in our analysis of domain names; we are, after all, dealing with the same marks, the same products and services, the same consumers, etc. Disposing of the issue so readily, however, would ignore the fact that the likelihood of confusion in the domain name context resulted largely from the associational confusion between West Coast's domain name "moviebuff.com" and Brookfield's trademark "MovieBuff." The question in the meta-tags context is quite different. Here, we must determine whether West Coast can use "MovieBuff" or"moviebuff.com" in the meta-tags of its web site at "westcoastvideo.com" or at any other domain address *other than* "moviebuff.com" (which we have determined that West Coast may not use).

Although entering "MovieBuff" into a search engine is likely to bring up a list including "westcoastvideo.com" if West Coast has included that term in its meta-tags, the resulting confusion is not as great as where West Coast uses the "moviebuff.com" domain name. First, when the user inputs "MovieBuff" into an Internet search engine, the list produced by the search engine is likely to include both West Coast's and Brookfield's web sites. Thus, in scanning such list, the Web user will often be able to find the particular web site he is seeking. Moreover, even if the web user chooses the web site belonging to West Coast, he will see that the domain name of the web site he selected is "westcoast-video.com." Since there is no confusion resulting from the domain address, and since West Coast's initial web page prominently displays its own name, it is difficult to say that a consumer is likely to be confused about whose site he has reached or to think that Brookfield somehow sponsors West Coast's web site.

Nevertheless, West Coast's use of "moviebuff.com" in meta-tags will still result in what is known as initial interest confusion. Web surfers looking for Brookfield's "MovieBuff" products who are taken by a search engine to "westcoastvideo.com" will find a database similar enough to "MovieBuff" such that a sizeable number of consumers who were originally looking for Brook-field's product will simply decide to utilize West Coast's offerings instead. Although there is no source confusion in the sense that consumers know they are patronizing West Coast rather than Brookfield, there is nevertheless initial interest confusion in the sense that, by using "moviebuff.com" or "MovieBuff" to divert people looking for "MovieBuff" to its web site, West Coast improperly benefits from the goodwill that Brookfield developed in its mark. Recently in *Dr. Seuss*, we explicitly recognized that the use of another's trademark in a manner calculated "to capture initial consumer attention, even though no actual sale is finally completed as a result of the confusion, may be still an infringement." *Dr. Seuss, 109 F.3d at 1405.*

The *Dr. Seuss* court, in recognizing that the diversion of consumers' initial interest is a form of confusion against which the Lanham Act protects, relied upon *Mobil Oil*. In that case, Mobil Oil Corporation ("Mobil") asserted a federal trademark infringement claim against Pegasus Petroleum, alleging that Pegasus Petroleum's use of "Pegasus" was likely to cause confusion with Mobil's trade-mark, a flying horse symbol in the form of the Greek mythological Pegasus. Mobil established that "potential purchasers would be misled into an initial interest in Pegasus Petroleum" because they thought that Pegasus Petroleum was associated with Mobil. But these potential customers would generally learn that Pegasus Petroleum was unrelated to Mobil well before any actual sale was consummated. Nevertheless, the Second Circuit held that "such initial confusion works a sufficient trademark injury."

Mobil Oil relied upon its earlier opinion in *Grotrian, Helfferich, Schulz, Th. Steinweg Nachf. v. Steinway & Sons, 523 F.2d 1331, 1341-42 (2d Cir. 1975).* Analyzing the plaintiff's claim that the defendant, through its use of the "Grotrian-Steinweg" mark, attracted people really interested in plaintiff's "Steinway" pianos, the Second Circuit explained:

> We decline to hold, however, that actual or potential confusion at the time of purchase necessarily must be demonstrated to establish trademark infringe-ment under the circumstances of this case.
>
> The issue here is not the possibility that a purchaser would buy a Grotrian-Steinweg thinking it was actually a Steinway or that Grotrian had some con-nection with Steinway and Sons. The harm to Steinway, rather, is the likelihood that a consumer, hearing the "Grotrian-Steinweg" name and thinking it had some connection with "Steinway," would consider it on that basis. The "Gro-trian-Steinweg" name therefore would attract potential customers based on the reputation built up by Steinway in this country for many years. *Grotrian, 523 F.2d at 1342.*

Both *Dr. Seuss* and the Second Circuit hold that initial interest confusion is actionable under the Lanham Act, which holdings are bolstered by the decisions of many other courts which have similarly recognized that the federal trademark and unfair competition laws do protect against this form of consumer confusion.

Using another's trademark in one's meta-tags is much like posting a sign with another's trademark in front of one's store. Suppose West Coast's competitor (let's call it "Blockbuster") puts up a billboard on a highway reading—"West Coast Video: 2 miles ahead at Exit 7"—where West Coast is really located at Exit 8 but Blockbuster is located at Exit 7. Customers looking for West Coast's store will pull off at Exit 7 and drive around looking for it. Unable to locate West Coast, but seeing the Blockbuster store right by the highway entrance, they may simply rent there. Even consumers who prefer West Coast may find it not worth the trouble to continue searching for West Coast since there is a Blockbuster right there. Customers are not confused in the narrow sense: they are fully aware that they are purchasing from Blockbuster and they have no reason to believe that Blockbuster is related to, or in any way sponsored by, West Coast. Nevertheless, the fact that there is only initial consumer confusion does not alter the fact that Blockbuster would be misappropriating West Coast's acquired goodwill.

The few courts to consider whether the use of another's trademark in one's meta-tags constitutes trademark infringement have ruled in the affirmative. For example, in a case in which Playboy Enterprises, Inc. ("Playboy") sued AsiaFocus International, Inc. ("AsiaFocus") for trademark infringement resulting from AsiaFocus's use of the federally registered trademarks "Playboy" and "Playmate" in its HTML code, a district court granted judgment in Playboy's favor, reasoning that AsiaFocus intentionally misled viewers into believing that its web site was connected with, or sponsored by, Playboy.

In a similar case also involving Playboy, a district court in California concluded that Playboy had established a likelihood of success on the merits of its claim that defendants' repeated use of "Playboy" within "machine readable code in Defendants' Internet web pages, so that the PLAYBOY trademark [was] accessible to individuals or Internet search engines which attempted to access Plaintiff under Plaintiff's PLAYBOY registered trademark" constituted trademark infringement. The court accordingly enjoined the defendants from using Playboy's marks in buried code or meta-tags.

In a meta-tags case with an interesting twist, a district court in Massachusetts also enjoined the use of meta-tags in a manner that resulted in initial interest confusion. *See Niton, 27 F. Supp. 2d at 102-05.* In that case, the defendant Radiation Monitoring Devices (RMD) did not simply use Niton Corporation's ("Niton") trademark in its meta-tags. Instead, RMD's web site directly copied Niton's web site's meta-tags and HTML code. As a result, whenever a search performed on an Internet search engine listed Niton's web site, it also listed RMD's site. Although the opinion did not speak in terms of initial consumer confusion, the court made clear that its issuance of preliminary injunctive relief was based on the fact that RMD was purposefully diverting people looking for Niton to its web site.

Consistently with *Dr. Seuss*, the Second Circuit, and the cases which have addressed trademark infringement through meta-tags use, we conclude that the Lanham Act bars West Coast from including in its meta-tags any term confusingly similar with Brookfield's mark. West Coast argues that our holding conflicts with *Holiday Inns*, in which the Sixth Circuit held that there was no trademark infringement where an alleged infringer merely took advantage of a situation in which confusion was likely to exist and did not affirmatively act to create consumer confusion. Unlike the defendant in *Holiday Inns*, however, West Coast was not a passive figure; instead, it acted affirmatively in placing Brookfield's trademark in the meta-tags of its web site, thereby *creating* the initial interest confusion. Accordingly, our conclusion comports with *Holiday Inns*.

C

Contrary to West Coast's contentions, we are not in any way restricting West Coast's right to use terms in a manner which would constitute fair use under the Lanham Act. It is well established that the Lanham Act does not prevent one from using a competitor's mark truthfully to identify the competitor's goods, or in comparative advertisements. This fair use doctrine applies in cyberspace as it does in the real world.

In *Welles*, the case most on point, Playboy sought to enjoin former Playmate of the Year Terri Welles ("Welles") from using "Playmate" or "Playboy" on her web site featuring photographs of herself. Welles' web site advertised the fact that she was a former Playmate of the Year, but minimized the use of Playboy's marks; it also contained numerous disclaimers stating that her site was neither endorsed by nor affiliated with Playboy. The district court found that Welles was using "Playboy" and "Playmate" not as trademarks, but rather as descriptive terms fairly and accurately describing her web page, and that her use of "Playboy" and "Playmate" in her web site's meta-tags was a permissible, good-faith attempt to index the content of her web site. It accordingly concluded that her use was permissible under the trademark laws.

We agree that West Coast can legitimately use an appropriate descriptive term in its meta-tags. But "MovieBuff" is not such a descriptive term. Even though it differs from "Movie Buff" by only a single space, that difference is pivotal. The term "Movie Buff" is a descriptive term, which is routinely used in the English language to describe a movie devotee. "MovieBuff" is not. The term "MovieBuff" is not in the dictionary. Nor has that term been used in any published federal or state court opinion. In light of the fact that it is not a word in the English language, when the term "MovieBuff" *is* employed, it is used to refer to Brookfield's products and services, rather than to mean "motion picture enthusiast." The proper term for the "motion picture enthusiast" is "Movie Buff," which West Coast certainly *can* use. It cannot, however, omit the space.

Moreover, West Coast is not absolutely barred from using the term "MovieBuff." As we explained above, that term can be legitimately used to describe Brookfield's product. For example, its web page might well include an advertisement banner such as "Why pay for MovieBuff when you can get the same thing here for FREE?" which clearly employs "MovieBuff" to refer to Brookfield's products. West Coast, however, presently uses Brookfield's trademark not to reference Brookfield's products, but instead to describe its own product (in the case of the domain name) and to attract people to its web site (in the case of the meta-tags). That is not fair use.

Part VI

Having concluded that Brookfield has established a likelihood of success on the merits of its trademark infringement claim, we analyze the other requirement for preliminary injunctive relief inquiry, irreparable injury. Although the district court did not address this issue, irreparable injury may be presumed from a showing of likelihood of success on the merits of a trademark infringement claim. Preliminary injunctive relief is appropriate here to prevent irreparable injury to Brookfield's interests in its trademark "MovieBuff" and to promote the public interest in protecting trademarks generally as well.

Part VII

As we have seen, registration of a domain name for a web site does not trump long-established principles of trademark law. When a firm uses a competitor's trademark in the domain name of its web site, users are likely to be confused as to its source or sponsorship. Similarly, using a competitor's trademark in the meta-tags of such web site is likely to cause what we have described as initial interest confusion. These forms of confusion are exactly what the trademark laws are designed to prevent.

Accordingly, we reverse and remand this case to the district court with instructions to enter a preliminary injunction in favor of Brookfield in accordance with this opinion.

Reversed and Remanded.

Appendix B

PACCAR, Inc., Plaintiff, v. TeleScan Technologies, L.L.C., Defendant

115 F. Supp. 2d 772 (E.D. Michigan, 2000)

Opinion: Memorandum and Order Granting Preliminary Injunction

I. Introduction

This is a trademark infringement case. Plaintiff PACCAR, Inc. ("PACCAR") owns a number of U.S. trademark registrations for the marks "Peterbilt" and "Kenworth." PACCAR is suing defendant TeleScan Technologies, L.L.C. ("TeleScan") for trademark infringement and trademark dilution for TeleScan's use of PACCAR's trademarks within several of TeleScan's web site domain names. Now before the Court is PACCAR's motion for a preliminary injunction (1) enjoining TeleScan from using the names "Peterbilt" and "Kenworth" in any of TeleScan's domain names, meta-tags, web pages, or web sites, and (2) causing TeleScan to transfer registration and ownership of the domain names containing "Peterbilt" and "Kenworth" to PACCAR. For the reasons that follow, the mo-tion will be granted.

II. Facts

A. The Parties

1. PACCAR is a manufacturer of heavy trucks and truck parts under the "Peterbilt" and "Kenworth" trademarks. Peterbilt Motors Company and Kenworth Truck Company, both divisions of PACCAR, have been manufacturing trucks under their respective names for over fifty years. PACCAR has invested substantial amounts of money in developing, marketing, and advertising the Peterbilt and Kenworth marks. PACCAR permits authorized Peterbilt and Kenworth dealers to use the Peterbilt and Kenworth marks in their businesses. PACCAR has not licensed or authorized TeleScan to use the Peterbilt and Kenworth marks.

In addition to its manufacturing business, PACCAR administers a used truck locator service on its web site, found at www.paccar.com. This service allows consumers to search a database of Peterbilt and Kenworth trucks available for sale from Peterbilt and Kenworth dealers using 12 different search fields including model, year, and location.

2. TeleScan is the owner of several web sites providing truck locator services, including one found at www.truckscan.com. Using the "truckscan.com" web site, consumers can search for new and used trucks either by viewing listings by dealer, or by searching a database of the participating

dealers using eleven different search terms. Presumably, the individual dealers pay TeleScan to be included on its web sites and in its databases.

Another of TeleScan's web sites, found at www.telescanequipment.com, provides consumers with manufacturer-specific links to TeleScan's other web sites such as those found at, *inter alia*:

www.peterbilttrucks.com, www.peterbiltnewtrucks.com,
www.peterbiltusedtrucks.com, www.peterbiltdealers.com,
www.peterbilttruckdealers.com, www.kenworthnewtrucks.com,
www.kenworthusedtrucks.com, www.kenworthdealers.com, and
www.kenworthtruckdealers.com (domain names).

(For reasons unknown to the Court, these manufacturer-specific web sites appear to be currently out of service.) In addition to being linked to the telescanequipment.com web site, the manufacturer-specific web sites can also be accessed independently by using their domain name address. On the manufacturer-specific web sites, there are links to listings of the particular manufacturer's trucks and dealers. There is also a disclaimer on each manufacturer-specific web site which states: "This website provides a listing service for name brand products and has no affiliation with any manufacturer whose branded products are listed here."

B. Domain Names and the Internet

The Ninth Circuit recently gave an excellent description of the Internet and domain names, as follows:

The Internet is a global network of interconnected computers which allows users around the world to communicate and share information. The Web, a collection of information resources contained in documents located on individual computers around the world, is the most widely used and fastest-growing part of the Internet, except perhaps for electronic mail ("e-mail"). With the Web becoming an important mechanism for commerce, companies are racing to stake out their place in cyberspace. Prevalent on the web are multimedia "web pages" [or web sites]—computer data files written in Hypertext Markup Language (HTML)—which contain information such as text, pictures, sounds, audio and video recordings, and links to other web pages.

Each web page has a corresponding domain address, which is an identifier somewhat analogous to a telephone number or street address. Domain names consist of a second-level domain—simply a term or series of terms (e.g., westcoastvideo)—followed by a top-level domain, many of which describe the nature of the enterprise. Top-level domains include ".com" (commercial), ".edu" (educational), ".org" (non-profit and miscellaneous organizations), ".gov" (government), ".net" (networking provider), and ".mil" (military). Commercial entities generally use the ".com" top-level domain, which also serves as a catch-all top-level domain. . . . Each web page must have a unique domain name. . . .

Using a Web browser, such as Netscape's Navigator or Microsoft's Internet Explorer, a cyber "surfer" may navigate the Web—searching for, communicating with, and retrieving information from various web sites. A specific web site is most easily located by using its domain name. Upon entering a domain name into the web browser, the corresponding web site will quickly appear on the computer screen. Sometimes, however, a Web surfer will not know the domain name of the site he is looking for, whereupon he has two principal options: trying to guess the domain name, or seeking the assistance of an Internet "search engine" [such as Yahoo!].

Oftentimes, an Internet user will begin by hazarding a guess at the domain name, especially if there is an obvious domain name to try. Web users often assume, as a rule of thumb, that the domain name of a particular company will be the company name followed by ".com." . . . Sometimes, a trademark is better known than the company itself, in which case a web surfer may assume that the domain address will be "'trademark'.com.". . .

A Web surfer's second option when he does not know the domain name is to utilize an Internet search engine, such as Yahoo, Altavista, or Lycos. When a keyword is entered, the search engine processes it through a self-created index of web sites to generate a (sometimes long) list relating to the entered keyword. Each search engine uses its own algorithm to arrange indexed materials in sequence, so the list of web sites that any particular set of keywords will bring up may differ depending on the search engine used. Search engines look for keywords in places such a domain names, actual text on the web page, and meta-tags. Meta-tags are HTML code intended to describe the contents of the web site. There are different types of meta-tags, but those of principal concern to us are the "description" and "keyword" meta-tags. The description meta-tags are intended to describe the web site; the keyword meta-tags, at least in theory, contain keywords relating to the contents of the web site. The more often a term appears in the meta-tags and in the text of the web page, the more likely it is that the web page will be "hit" in a search for that keyword and the higher on the list of "hits" the web page will appear. *Brookfield Comm. v. West Coast Entertainment Corp., 174 F.3d 1036, 1044-45 (9th Cir. 1999).*

III. Analysis

A. Likelihood of Confusion

PACCAR asserts claims for trademark infringement and trademark dilution under the Lanham Act, *15 U.S.C. § 1114* and § 1125.

1. Trademark Infringement

a. Standard

"The touchstone of liability under § 1114 is whether the defendant's use of the disputed mark is likely to cause confusion among consumers regarding the origin of the goods offered by the parties." *Daddy's Junky Music Stores, Inc. v. Big Daddy's Family Music Ctr., 109 F.3d 275, 280 (6th Cir. 1997).* This is determined by a consideration of the following factors: (1) strength of the plaintiff's mark, (2) relatedness of the goods or services, (3) similarity of the marks, (4) evidence of actual confusion, (5) marketing channels used, (6) likely degree of purchaser care, (7) defendant's intent in selecting its mark, and (8) likelihood of expansion of the product lines. *Frisch's Restaurants, Inc. v. Elby's Big Boy of Steubenville, Inc., 670 F.2d 642, 648 (6th Cir. 1982).* These factors must be considered together and "imply no mathematical precision." *Wynn Oil Co. v. Thomas, 839 F.2d 1183, 1186 (6th Cir. 1988).* In fact, "a plaintiff need not show that all, or even most of the factors listed are present in any particular case to be significant." *Id.* The ultimate question is merely "whether relevant consumers are likely to believe that the products or services offered by the parties are affiliated in some way." *Daddy's Junky Music, supra at 280.*

b. Strength of Marks

Peterbilt and Kenworth are very strong marks which have been used nationwide to indicate a certain manufacturer of trucks for decades. The marks were derived as variations of the names of the original developers and fall into the categories of fanciful and arbitrary. Also, defendant does not challenge the strength or distinction of the Peterbilt and Kenworth marks. Thus, PACCAR's marks are entitled to the highest protection.

c. Similarity of Marks

TeleScan's domain names are very similar to PACCAR's marks. In each domain name, there is an exact character match to both the Peterbilt and Kenworth marks (e.g. peterbilttrucks.com, kenworthusedtrucks.com). Moreover, the mere addition of characters following the marks does not eliminate the likelihood of confusion here.

In *Minnesota Mining & Mfg. Co. v. Taylor, 21 F. Supp. 2d 1003 (D. Minn. 1998),* the court granted a preliminary injunction against the unauthorized use of the trademark "Post-It," in the domain names, ipost-it.com and post-its.com. Similarly, in *Playboy Enter., Inc. v. AsiaFocus Int'l, Inc., 1998 U.S. Dist.* (E.D. Va. April 10, 1998) (unpublished), the domain names, playmates-asian.com and asian-playmates.com, were held to infringe upon and dilute the "Playmate" trademark. The district court stated: "although the defendants' use of the term 'playmate' as the main component of the domain names . . . did not exactly duplicate [plaintiff's] mark, minor differences between the registered mark and the unauthorized use of the mark do not preclude liability under the Lanham Act." Also, in a recent Uniform Domain Name Dispute Resolution Policy (UDRP) proceeding, the domain names, kenworthtruck.com and kenworthalley.com, were determined to be likely to cause confusion with PACCAR's marks. *PACCAR Inc. v. Enyart Assoc., WIPO Arbitration and Mediation Center, Case No. D2000-0289 (May 26, 2000).*

Further, the Court of Appeals for the Sixth Circuit has recognized, outside of the domain name context, that slight modifications to a trademark do not necessarily preclude infringement. In *Induct-O-Matic Corp. v. Inductotherm Corp., 747 F.2d 358, 363-64 (6th Cir. 1984),* the Sixth Circuit held that the addition of a descriptive term like "matic" does not distinguish the "induct-o-matic" from the trademark "inducto," and that the two were therefore "deceptively similar."

Here, like in *Induct-O-Matic, supra,* the additions of "truck," "newtrucks," or "usedtrucks" to the marks Peterbilt or Kenworth, do not distinguish TeleScan's domain names from PACCAR's marks. Because Peterbilt and Kenworth are so closely associated with trucks, "peterbilttrucks.com" is not appreciably different from "peterbilt.com."

d. Relatedness of Goods and Service

The goods and services provided by PACCAR and TeleScan are closely related. TeleScan's contention, that it is not in competition with anything that PACCAR provides because PACCAR is not in the business of selling used trucks, is not well received. PACCAR and TeleScan both offer a used-truck locator database through the Internet. Also, TeleScan employs the domain names specifically to provide services related to PACCAR's products—locating new and used Peterbilt and Kenworth trucks for sale.

e. Actual Confusion

There has been no submission of any evidence showing actual confusion here. However, while the presence of actual confusion in a case is strong evidence for the plaintiff, the absence of such evidence is not dispositive.

f. Marketing Channels

Both PACCAR and TeleScan market their goods and services through the Internet, which increases the likelihood of confusion between the two marks. As was noted by the Ninth Circuit in *Brookfield, supra,* simultaneous use of the Internet as a marketing and advertising tool renders it more likely that customer confusion will result. Because of the ease in which the Internet allows users to surf for information, "Web surfers are more likely to be confused as to the ownership of a web site than traditional patrons of a brick-and-mortar store would be of a store's ownership." *Brookfield, 174 F.3d at 1057.* Also, because the marks Peterbilt and Kenworth are in the domain names of TeleScan's web sites, as opposed to simply being shown on the web page itself, a consumer is likely to mistakenly believe that PACCAR sponsored the web site and database, or that they are related companies.

Moreover, the presence of a disclaimer on TeleScan's web sites does not remedy any infringement caused by an improper domain name. An infringing domain name has the potential to misdirect consumers as they look for web sites associated with the owner of a trademark. A disclaimer that purports to disavow association with the trademark owner after the consumer has reached the site comes too late; the customer has already been misdirected. This problem, denoted as "initial interest confusion," and recognized by at least one case in this district, is a form of confusion protected by the Lanham Act. *Brookfield, 174 F.3d at 1062-63.*

g. Customer Care

Despite TeleScan's argument that truck dealers, per se, are sophisticated purchasers who will not be easily confused, the relevant customer in this circumstance is an average Internet user, not a sophisticated truck dealer. This is because the type of confusion engendered by infringing domain names results because "Internet users do not undergo a highly sophisticated analysis when searching for domain names." *Green Products Co., supra at 1079.* Accordingly, the degree of customer care here favors a likelihood of confusion.

h. TeleScan's Intent

(i)

TeleScan contends that it did not adopt PACCAR's trademarks to intentionally cause confusion, or for the sole purpose of selling it to a rightful trademark owner. Rather, it argues that it uses the marks Peterbilt and Kenworth in a purely descriptive sense—the domain names simply describe what is on their respective web sites (e.g., the "peterbiltusedtrucks.com" web site contains a listing of used Peterbilt trucks for sale). TeleScan analogizes its use of the Peterbilt and Kenworth marks in its domain names to classified advertising. Relying heavily on *Volkswagen, A.G. v. Church, 411 F.2d 350 (9th Cir. 1969),* where the Ninth Circuit held that use of a trademark in advertising a repair service constituted a fair use, TeleScan argues that its use of PACCAR's trademarks is a fair use under trademark law.

TeleScan's analogy, as revealed by its statement, "Thus, the Defendant's use of Plaintiff's trademark in its web page to sell products of truck dealers is fair use," is defective. Defendant's brief in response at p. 7 (emphasis added). Here, TeleScan goes beyond merely using the Peterbilt and Kenworth marks on its web page; it uses them in its domain name. Due to the nature of the Internet, and the way in which Internet surfers search for information on the Web, a domain name is significantly different than a classified advertisement. The use of the name of a truck in a classified advertisement communicates information as to the source of the truck, not information as to the seller of the truck. Words in domain names, however, do communicate information as to the nature of the entity sponsoring the web site. Using the name Peterbilt or Kenworth in a domain name sends a message to Internet users that the web site is associated with, or sponsored by the company owning the trademarks Peterbilt and Kenworth. TeleScan's arguments essentially confuse the nature of what its domain names describe; the domain names here describe the web site, not the trucks. Consequently, it is not a fair use.

(ii)

The undisputed evidence also indicates that even if TeleScan did not adopt the domain names with the purposeful intent to deceive the public, it certainly intended to derive a benefit from the reputation of the Peterbilt and Kenworth marks. Simply using a contested mark with knowledge of the protected mark at issue can support a finding of intentional copy. Here, TeleScan put the words Peterbilt and Kenworth into its domain names solely because they were associated with Peterbilt and Kenworth trucks. Also, looking at the web pages themselves, the words Peterbilt and Kenworth are used repetitively, in both the main title and in a "wallpaper" that underlies the entire page, and are displayed in fonts that are similar to the fonts in PACCAR's trademarks (i.e., cursive script for Peterbilt and block script for Kenworth). Moreover, the words Peterbilt and Kenworth are included in the meta-tags of the web sites, which makes it more likely an Internet search engine will "hit" the web sites in response to searches using Peterbilt or Kenworth as keywords. Thus, TeleScan's use of the Peterbilt and Kenworth marks in its domain names, and meta-tags, increase the likelihood that someone looking for a Peterbilt or Kenworth truck specifically, will come upon TeleScan's web sites first, thereby increasing the value of its web site.

i. Expansion into Product Lines

Both parties already occupy the same field of locating used-trucks via the Internet, so this factor is irrelevant.

j. Summary

In sum, there is a strong likelihood of confusion present here. As such, PACCAR has adequately proven its trademark infringement claim.

2. Trademark Dilution

Trademark dilution is defined as the "lessening of the capacity of a famous mark to identify and distinguish goods or services. . . ." *15 U.S.C. § 1127.* A finding of a likelihood of confusion is not a necessary element for a claim of trademark dilution. Id.; *15 U.S.C. § 1125.* Rather, the harm is "the inability of the victim to control the nature and quality of the defendant's goods." *Intermatic, Inc. v. Toeppen, 947 F. Supp. 1227, 1240 (N.D. Ill. 1996).* In the context of domain names, it has been held that the use of another's trademark in a domain names "dilutes" the trademark by placing the trademark owner "at the mercy" of the web site operator. The web site operator is able to decide what messages, goods, or services are associated with the web site and by extension, with the trademark.

TeleScan's only response to PACCAR's claim of trademark dilution is that there is no tarnishment or blurring of PACCAR's marks because the goods TeleScan sells are manufactured by PACCAR. Again, TeleScan's argument misses the point. The issue is the web site itself, not the trucks. Here, there is sufficient evidence to believe that a consumer may mistakenly associate TeleScan's web sites with PACCAR's trademarks. Since PACCAR has no power to influence or control what appears on TeleScan's web sites, it is effectively "at the mercy" of TeleScan. Thus, TeleScan's use of PACCAR's trademarks in TeleScan's domain names is trademark dilution.

B. Injury/Harm

In cases, such as here, where a likelihood of confusion is found, injury on the part of the trademark holder is presumed. Also, as noted previously, for at least one week prior to the date of this memo, TeleScan's web sites utilizing the Peterbilt and Kenworth names, were out of service. As such, this would indicate that TeleScan can function adequately without the contested domain names, and corresponding web sites. Moreover, some authority suggests that the use of trademarks in the post-domain path of a URL is acceptable (e.g., www.telescan.com/peterbilt). Thus, TeleScan could potentially maintain the same list of Peterbilt dealers, supported by its telescan.com web site, without using Peterbilt or Kenworth in the domain name itself. Therefore, the permanent injunction will not seriously or irreparably harm TeleScan.

C. Public Interest

It is in the public's interest to protect consumers from confusion and protect the right of a trademark owner to control its own product's reputation. Accordingly, it is in the public's interest to prevent Internet users' confusion over the contested web sites.

IV. Conclusion

For the reasons stated above, which constitute the Court's Findings of Fact and Conclusions of Law, PACCAR's motion for a preliminary injunction is granted as follows:

(1) TeleScan shall immediately take whatever steps are necessary, at its own expense, to cease and desist from using the following domain names, currently registered with Network Solutions, Inc., in any fashion or for any purpose:

(a) peterbilttrucks.com
(b) peterbiltnewtrucks.com
(c) peterbiltusedtrucks.com
(d) peterbiltdealers.com
(e) peterbilttruckdealers.com
(f) kenworthnewtrucks.com
(g) kenworthusedtrucks.com
(h) kenworthdealers.com
(i) kenworthtruckdealers.com

(2) TeleScan shall immediately take all actions necessary to transfer registration and ownership of the domain names, listed in subparagraph (1), to PACCAR.

(3) TeleScan is enjoined from using the Peterbilt and Kenworth trademarks, or any colorable imitation thereof, in any domain name or web page meta-tag.

(4) TeleScan is enjoined from using the Peterbilt or Kenworth trademarks, or any colorable imitation thereof, on its own web page(s) in a way such that it is likely to cause confusion on the part of consumers that the web page is associated with PACCAR, Peterbilt or Kenworth, including the use of the trademarks as the title or as "wallpaper" background of a web page.

(5) TeleScan shall post this Order on its web site(s) and give notice of it to all its customers, correspondents, members, and subscribers.

(6) TeleScan shall file with the Court and serve upon PACCAR's counsel, within 30 days, a report in writing and under oath setting forth in detail the manner and form in which TeleScan has complied with the requirements of this injunction.

The preliminary injunction does not extend to TeleScan's use of the Peterbilt and Kenworth trademarks on its own web page(s) in any other way consistent with this injunction.

A separate paper styled "Preliminary Injunction" will be filed simultaneously with this Order.

So Ordered.

Appendix C

Universal City Studios, Inc., et al., Plaintiffs, v. Shawn C. Reimerdes, et. al., Defendants

111 F. Supp. 2d 294 (S.D.N.Y, 2000)

Opinion: Lewis A. Kaplan, *District Judge.*

Plaintiffs, eight major United States motion picture studios, distribute many of their copyrighted motion pictures for home use on digital versatile disks (DVDs), which contain copies of the motion pictures in digital form. They protect those motion pictures from copying by using an encryption system called CSS. CSS-protected motion pictures on DVDs may be viewed only on players and computer drives equipped with licensed technology that permits the devices to decrypt and play—but not to copy—the films.

Late last year, computer hackers devised a computer program called DeCSS that circumvents the CSS protection system and allows CSS-protected motion pictures to be copied and played on devices that lack the licensed decryption technology. Defendants quickly posted DeCSS on their Internet web site, thus making it readily available to much of the world. Plaintiffs promptly brought this action under the Digital Millennium Copyright Act ("the DMCA") to enjoin defendants from posting DeCSS and to prevent them from electronically "linking" their site to others that post DeCSS. Defendants responded with what they termed "electronic civil disobedience"—increasing their efforts to link their web site to a large number of others that continue to make DeCSS available.

Defendants contend that their actions do not violate the DMCA and, in any case, that the DMCA, as applied to computer programs, or code, violates the First Amendment. This is the Court's decision after trial, and the decision may be summarized in a nutshell.

Defendants argue first that the DMCA should not be construed to reach their conduct, principally because the DMCA, so applied, could prevent those who wish to gain access to technologically protected copyrighted works in order to make fair—that is, non-infringing—use of them from doing so. They argue that those who would make fair use of technologically protected copyrighted works need means, such as DeCSS, of circumventing access control measures not for piracy, but to make lawful use of those works.

Technological access control measures have the capacity to prevent fair uses of copyrighted works as well as foul. Hence, there is a potential tension between the use of such access control measures and fair use. Defendants are not the first to recognize that possibility. As the DMCA made its way through the legislative process, Congress was preoccupied with precisely this issue. Proponents of strong restrictions on circumvention of access control measures argued that they were essential if copyright holders were to make their works available in digital form because digital works otherwise could be pirated too easily. Opponents contended that strong anticircumvention measures would extend the copyright monopoly inappropriately and prevent many fair uses of copyrighted material.

Congress struck a balance. The compromise it reached, depending upon future technological and commercial developments, may or may not prove ideal. But the solution it enacted is clear. The potential tension to which defendants point does not absolve them of liability under the statute. There is no serious question that defendants' posting of DeCSS violates the DMCA.

Defendants' constitutional argument ultimately rests on two propositions—that computer code, regardless of its function, is "speech" entitled to maximum constitutional protection and that computer code therefore essentially is exempt from regulation by government. But their argument is baseless.

Computer code is expressive. To that extent, it is a matter of First Amendment concern. But computer code is not purely expressive any more than the assassination of a political figure is purely a political statement. Code causes computers to perform desired functions. Its expressive element no more immunizes its functional aspects from regulation than the expressive motives of an assassin immunize the assassin's action.

In an era in which the transmission of computer viruses—which, like DeCSS, are simply computer code and thus to some degree expressive—can disable systems upon which the nation depends and in which other computer code also is capable of inflicting other harm, society must be able to regulate the use and dissemination of code in appropriate circumstances. The Constitution, after all, is a framework for building a just and democratic society. It is not a suicide pact.

I. The Genesis of the Controversy

As this case involves computers and technology with which many are unfamiliar, it is useful to begin by defining some of the vocabulary.

A. The Vocabulary of this Case

1. Computers and Operating Systems

A computer is "a digital information processing device . . . consisting of central processing components . . . and mass data storage . . . certain peripheral input/output devices . . . , and an operating system." Personal computers (PCs) are computers designed for use by one person at a time. "More powerful, more expensive computer systems known as 'servers' . . . are designed to provide data, services, and functionality through a digital network to multiple users." *U.S. v Microsoft, 84 F. Supp. 2d 9 (D.D.C., 1999).*

An operating system is "a software program that controls the allocation and use of computer resources (such as central processing unit time, main memory space, disk space, and input/output channels). The operating system also supports the functions of software programs, called 'applications,' that perform specific user-oriented tasks. . . . Because it supports applications while interacting more closely with the PC system's hardware, the operating system is said to serve as a 'platform.'" *United States v. Microsoft Corp., 84 F. Supp. 2d at 13.*

Microsoft Windows ("Windows") is an operating system released by Microsoft Corp. It is the most widely used operating system for PCs in the United States, and its versions include Windows 95, Windows 98, Windows NT and Windows 2000.

Linux, which was and continues to be developed through the open source model of software development, also is an operating system. It can be run on a PC as an alternative to Windows, although the extent to which it is so used is limited. Linux is more widely used on servers.

2. Computer Code

"Computers come down to one basic premise: They operate with a series of on and off switches, using two digits in the binary (base 2) number system—0 (for off) and 1 (for on)." *The New York Public Library, Science Desk Reference 496 (1995)* All data and instructions input to or contained in computers therefore must be reduced the numerals 1 and 0.

"The smallest unit of memory in a computer," a bit, "is a switch with a value of 0 (off) or 1 (on)." *Science Desk Reference, at 501.* A group of eight bits is called a byte and represents a character—a letter or an integer. A kilobyte (K) is 1024 bytes, a megabyte (MB) 1024 kilobytes, and a gigabyte (GB) 1024 megabytes.

Some highly skilled human beings can reduce data and instructions to strings of 1's and 0's and thus program computers to perform complex tasks by inputting commands and data in that form. But it would be inconvenient, inefficient and, for most people, probably impossible to do so. In consequence, computer science has developed programming languages. These languages, like other written languages, employ symbols and syntax to convey meaning. The text of programs written in these languages is referred to as source code. And whether directly or through the medium of another program, the sets of instructions written in programming languages—the source code—ultimately are translated into machine "readable" strings of 1's and 0's, known in the computer world as object code, which typically are executable by the computer.

The distinction between source and object code is not as crystal clear as first appears. Depending upon the programming language, source code may contain many 1's and 0's and look a lot like object code or may contain many instructions derived from spoken human language. Programming languages the source code for which approaches object code are referred to as low level source code while those that are more similar to spoken language are referred to as high level source code.

All code is human readable. As source code is closer to human language than is object code, it tends to be comprehended more easily by humans than object code.

3. The Internet and the World Wide Web

The Internet is "a global electronic network, consisting of smaller, interconnected networks, which allows millions of computers to exchange information over telephone wires, dedicated data cables, and wireless links. The Internet links PCs by means of servers, which run specialized operating systems and applications designed for servicing a network environment." *United States v. Microsoft Corp., 84 F. Supp. 2d at 13.*

Internet Relay Chat (IRC) is a system that enables individuals connected to the Internet to participate in live typed discussions. Participation in an IRC discussion requires an IRC software program, which sends messages via the Internet to the IRC server, which in turn broadcasts the messages to all participants. The IRC system is capable of supporting many separate discussions at once.

The World Wide Web (the "Web") is "a massive collection of digital information resources stored on servers throughout the Internet. These resources are typically provided in the form of hypertext documents, commonly referred to as 'web pages,' that may incorporate any combination of text, graphics, audio and video content, software programs, and other data. A user of a computer connected to the Internet can publish a page on the web simply by copying it into a specially designated, publicly accessible directory on a web server. Some web resources are in the form of applications that provide functionality through a user's PC system but actually execute on a server." *Id.*

A web site is "a collection of web pages [published on the web by an individual or organization] . . . . Most web pages are in the form of 'hypertext'; that is, they contain annotated references, or 'hyperlinks,' to other web pages. Hyperlinks can be used as cross-references within a single document, between documents on the same site, or between documents on different sites." *Id at 14.*

A home page is "one page on each web site . . . [that typically serves as] the first access point to the site. The home page is usually a hypertext document that presents an overview of the site and hyperlinks to the other pages comprising the site." *Id.*

A web client is "software that, when running on a computer connected to the Internet, sends information to and receives information from web servers throughout the Internet. Web clients and servers transfer data using a standard known as the Hypertext Transfer Protocol (HTTP). A 'web browser' is a type of web client that enables a user to select, retrieve, and perceive resources on the web. In particular, web browsers provide a way for a user to view hypertext documents and follow the hyperlinks that connect them, typically by moving the cursor over a link and depressing the mouse button." *Id.*

4. Portable Storage Media

Digital files may be stored on several different kinds of storage media, some of which are readily transportable. Perhaps the most familiar of these are so called floppy disks or "floppies," which now are 3 1/2 inch magnetic disks upon which digital files may be recorded. For present purposes, however, we are concerned principally with two more recent developments, CD-ROMs and digital versatile disks, or DVDs.

A CD-ROM is a five-inch wide optical disk capable of storing approximately 650 MB of data. To read the data on a CD-ROM, a computer must have a CD-ROM drive.

DVDs are five-inch wide disks capable of storing more than 4.7 GB of data. In the application relevant here, they are used to hold full-length motion pictures in digital form. They are the latest technology for private home viewing of recorded motion pictures and result in drastically improved audio and visual clarity and quality of motion pictures shown on televisions or computer screens.

5. The Technology Here at Issue

CSS, or Content Scramble System, is an access control and copy prevention system for DVDs developed by the motion picture companies, including plaintiffs. It is an encryption-based system that requires the use of appropriately configured hardware such as a DVD player or a computer DVD drive to decrypt, unscramble and play back, but not copy, motion pictures on DVDs. The technology necessary to configure DVD players and drives to play CSS-protected DVDs has been licensed to hundreds of manufacturers in the United States and around the world.

DeCSS is a software utility, or computer program, that enables users to break the CSS copy protection system and hence to view DVDs on unlicensed players and make digital copies of DVD movies. The quality of motion pic-tures decrypted by DeCSS is virtually identical to that of encrypted movies on DVD.

DivX is a compression program available for download over the Internet. It compresses video files in order to minimize required storage space, often to facilitate transfer over the Internet or other networks.

B. Parties

Plaintiffs are eight major motion picture studios. Each is in the business of producing and distributing copyrighted material including motion pictures. Each distributes, either directly or through affiliates, copyrighted motion pictures on DVDs. Plaintiffs produce and distribute a large majority of the motion pictures on DVDs on the market today.

Defendant Eric Corley is viewed as a leader of the computer hacker community and goes by the name Emmanuel Goldstein, after the leader of the underground in George Orwell's classic, *1984*. He and his company, defendant 2600 Enterprises, Inc., together publish a magazine called *2600: The Hacker Quarterly*, which Corley founded in 1984, and which is something of a bible to the hacker community. The name "2600" was derived from the fact that hackers in the 1960's found that the transmission of a 2600 hertz tone over a long distance trunk connection gained access to "operator mode" and allowed the user to explore aspects of the telephone system that were not otherwise accessible. Mr. Corley chose the name because he regarded it as a "mystical thing," commemorating something that he evidently admired. Not surprisingly, *2600: The Hacker Quarterly* has included articles on such topics as how to steal an

Internet domain name, access other people's e-mail, intercept cellular phone calls, and break into the computer systems at Costco stores and Federal Express. One issue contains a guide to the federal criminal justice system for readers charged with computer hacking. In addition, defendants operate a web site located at http://www.2600.com ("2600.com"), which is managed primarily by Mr. Corley and has been in existence since 1995.

Prior to January 2000, when this action was commenced, defendants posted the source and object code for DeCSS on the 2600.com web site, from which they could be downloaded easily. At that time, 2600.com contained also a list of links to other web sites purporting to post DeCSS.

C. The Development of DVD and CSS

The major motion picture studios typically distribute films in a sequence of so-called windows, each window referring to a separate channel of distribution and thus to a separate source of revenue. The first window generally is theatrical release, distribution, and exhibition. Subsequently, films are distributed to airlines and hotels, then to the home market, then to pay television, cable and, eventually, free television broadcast. The home market is important to plaintiffs, as it represents a significant source of revenue.

Motion pictures first were, and still are, distributed to the home market in the form of video cassette tapes. In the early 1990s, however, the major movie studios began to explore distribution to the home market in digital format, which offered substantially higher audio and visual quality and greater longevity than video cassette tapes. This technology, which in 1995 became what is known today as DVD, brought with it a new problem—increased risk of piracy by virtue of the fact that digital files, unlike the material on video cassettes, can be copied without degradation from generation to generation. In consequence, the movie studios became concerned as the product neared market with the threat of DVD piracy.

Discussions among the studios with the goal of organizing a unified response to the piracy threat began in earnest in late 1995 or early 1996. They eventually came to include representatives of the consumer electronics and computer industries, as well as interested members of the public, and focused on both legislative proposals and technological solutions. In 1996, Matsushita Electric Industrial Co. (MEI) and Toshiba Corp., presented—and the studios adopted—CSS.

CSS involves encrypting, according to an encryption algorithm, the digital sound and graphics files on a DVD that together constitute a motion picture. A CSS-protected DVD can be decrypted by an appropriate decryption algorithm that employs a series of keys stored on the DVD and the DVD player. In consequence, only players and drives containing the appropriate keys are able to decrypt DVD files and thereby play movies stored on DVDs.

As the motion picture companies did not themselves develop CSS and, in any case, are not in the business of making DVD players and drives, the technology for making compliant devices, i.e., devices with CSS keys, had to be licensed to consumer electronics manufacturers. In order to ensure that the decryption technology did not become generally available and that compliant devices could not be used to copy as well as merely to play CSS-protected movies, the technology is licensed subject to strict security requirements. Moreover, manufacturers may not, consistent with their licenses, make equipment that would supply digital output that could be used in copying protected DVDs. Licenses to manufacture compliant devices are granted on a royalty-free basis subject only to an administrative fee. At the time of trial, licenses had been issued to numerous hardware and software manufacturers, including two companies that plan to release DVD players for computers running the Linux operating system.

With CSS in place, the studios introduced DVDs on the consumer market in early 1997. All or most of the motion pictures released on DVD were, and continue to be, encrypted with CSS technology. Over 4,000 motion pictures now have been released in DVD format in the United States, and movies are being issued on DVD at the rate of over 40 new titles per month in addition to re-releases of classic films. Currently, more than five million households in the United States own DVD players, and players are projected to be in ten percent of United States homes by the end of 2000.

DVDs have proven not only popular, but lucrative for the studios. Revenue from their sale and rental currently accounts for a substantial percentage of the movie studios' revenue from the home video market. Revenue from the home market, in turn, makes up a large percentage of the studios' total distribution revenue.

D. The Appearance of DeCSS

In late September 1999, Jon Johansen, a Norwegian subject then fifteen years of age, and two individuals he "met" under pseudonyms over the Internet, reverse engineered a licensed DVD player and discovered the CSS encryption algorithm and keys. They used this information to create DeCSS, a program capable of decrypting or "ripping" encrypted DVDs, thereby allowing playback on non-compliant computers as well as the copying of decrypted files to computer hard drives. Mr. Johansen then posted the executable code on his personal Internet web site and informed members of an Internet mailing list that he had done so. Neither Mr. Johansen nor his collaborators obtained a license from the DVD CCA.

Although Mr. Johansen testified at trial that he created DeCSS in order to make a DVD player that would operate on a computer running the Linux operating system, DeCSS is a Windows executable file; that is, it can be executed only on computers running the Windows operating system. Mr. Johansen explained the fact that he created a Windows rather than a Linux program by asserting that Linux, at the time he created DeCSS, did not support the file system used on DVDs. Hence, it was necessary, he said, to decrypt the DVD on a Windows computer in order subsequently to play the decrypted files on a Linux machine. Assuming that to be true, however, the fact remains that Mr. Johansen created DeCSS in the full knowledge that it could be used on computers running Windows rather than Linux. Moreover, he was well aware that the files, once decrypted, could be copied like any other computer files.

In January 1999, Norwegian prosecutors filed charges against Mr. Johansen stemming from the development of DeCSS. The disposition of the Norwegian case does not appear of record.

E. The Distribution of DeCSS

In the months following its initial appearance on Mr. Johansen's web site, DeCSS has become widely available on the Internet, where hundreds of sites now purport to offer the software for download. A few other applications said to decrypt CSS-encrypted DVDs also have appeared on the Internet.

In November 1999, defendants' web site began to offer DeCSS for download. It established also a list of links to several web sites that purportedly "mirrored" or offered DeCSS for download. The links on defendants' mirror list fall into one of three categories. By clicking the mouse on one of these links, the user may be brought to a page on the linked-to site on which there appears a further link to the DeCSS software. If the user then clicks on the DeCSS link, download of the software begins. This page may or may not contain content other than the DeCSS link. Alternatively, the user may be brought to a page on the linked-to site that does not itself purport to link to DeCSS, but that links, either directly or via a series of other pages on the site, to another page on the site on which there appears a link to the DeCSS software. Finally, the user may be brought directly to the DeCSS link on the linked-to site such that download of DeCSS begins immediately without further user intervention.

F. The Preliminary Injunction and Defendants' Response

The movie studios, through the Internet investigations division of the Motion Picture Association of America (MPAA), became aware of the availability of DeCSS on the Internet in October 1999. The industry responded by sending out a number of cease and desist letters to web site operators who posted the software, some of which removed it from their sites. In January 2000, the studios filed this lawsuit against defendant Eric Corley and two others.

After a hearing at which defendants presented no affidavits or evidentiary material, the Court granted plaintiffs' motion for a preliminary injunction barring defendants from posting DeCSS. At the conclusion of the hearing, plaintiffs sought also to enjoin defendants from linking to other sites that posted DeCSS, but the Court declined to entertain the application at that time in view of plaintiffs' failure to raise the issue in their motion papers.

Following the issuance of the preliminary injunction, defendants removed DeCSS from the 2600.com web site. In what they termed an act of "electronic civil disobedience," however, they continued to support links to other web sites purporting to offer DeCSS for download, a list which had grown to nearly five hundred by July 2000. Indeed, they carried a banner saying "Stop the MPAA" and, in a reference to this lawsuit, proclaimed:

"We have to face the possibility that we could be forced into submission. For that reason it's especially important that as many of you as possible, all throughout the world, take a stand and mirror these files." Thus, defendants obviously hoped to frustrate plaintiffs' recourse to the judicial system by making effective relief difficult or impossible.

At least some of the links currently on defendants' mirror list lead the user to copies of DeCSS that, when downloaded and executed, successfully decrypt a motion picture on a CSS-encrypted DVD.

G. Effects on Plaintiffs

The effect on plaintiffs of defendants' posting of DeCSS depends upon the ease with which DeCSS decrypts plaintiffs' copyrighted motion pictures, the quality of the resulting product, and the convenience with which decrypted copies may be transferred or transmitted.

As noted, DeCSS was available for download from defendants' web site and remains available from web sites on defendants' mirror list. Downloading is simple and quick—plaintiffs' expert did it in seconds. The program in fact decrypts at least some DVDs. Although the process is computationally intensive, plaintiffs' expert decrypted a store-bought copy of *Sleepless in Seattle* in twenty to fourty-five minutes. The copy is stored on the hard drive of the computer. The quality of the decrypted film is virtually identical to that of encrypted films on DVD. The decrypted file can be copied like any other.

The decryption of a CSS-protected DVD is only the beginning of the tale, as the decrypted file is very large—approximately 4.3 to 6 GB or more depending on the length of the film—and thus extremely cumbersome to transfer or to store on portable storage media. One solution to this problem, however, is DivX, a compression utility available on the Internet that is promoted as a means of compressing decrypted motion picture files to manageable size.

DivX is capable of compressing decrypted files constituting a feature length motion picture to approximately 650 MB at a compression ratio that involves little loss of quality. While the compressed sound and graphic files then must be synchronized, a tedious process that took plaintiffs' expert between 10 and 20 hours, the task is entirely feasible. Indeed, having compared a store-bought DVD with portions of a copy compressed and synchronized with DivX (which often are referred to as "DivX'd" motion pictures), the Court finds that the loss of quality, at least in some cases, is imperceptible or so nearly imperceptible as to be of no importance to ordinary consumers.

The fact that DeCSS-decrypted DVDs can be compressed satisfactorily to 650 MB is very important. A writeable CD-ROM can hold 650 MB. Hence, it is entirely feasible to decrypt a DVD with DeCSS, compress and synchronize it with DivX, and then make as many copies as one wishes by burning the resulting files onto writeable CD-ROMs, which are sold blank for about one dollar apiece. Indeed, even if one wished to use a lower compression ratio to improve quality, a film easily could be compressed to about 1.3 GB and burned onto two CD-ROMs. But the creation of pirated copies of copyrighted movies on writeable CD-ROMs, although significant, is not the principal focus of plaintiffs' concern, which is transmission of pirated copies over the Internet or other networks.

Network transmission of decrypted motion pictures raises somewhat more difficult issues because even 650 MB is a very large file that, depending upon the circumstances, may take a good deal of time to transmit. But there is tremendous variation in transmission times. Many home computers today have modems with a rated capacity of 56 kilobits per second. DSL lines, which increasingly are available to home and business users, offer transfer rates of 7 megabits per second. Cable modems also offer increased bandwidth. Student rooms in many universities are equipped with network connections rated at 10 megabits per second. Large institutions such as universities and major companies often have networks with backbones rated at 100 megabits per second. While effective transmission times generally are much lower than rated maximum capacities in consequence of traffic volume and other considerations, there are many environments in which very high transmission rates may be achieved. Hence, transmission times ranging from three to twenty minutes to six hours or more for a feature length film are readily achievable, depending upon the users' precise circumstances.

At trial, defendants repeated, as if it were a mantra, the refrain that plaintiffs, as they stipulated, have no direct evidence of a specific occasion on which any person decrypted a copyrighted motion picture with DeCSS and transmitted it over the Internet. But that is unpersuasive. Plaintiffs' expert expended very little effort to find someone in an IRC chat room who exchanged a compressed, decrypted copy of *The Matrix*, one of plaintiffs' copyrighted motion pictures, for a copy of *Sleepless in Seattle*. While the simultaneous electronic exchange of the two movies took approximately six hours, the computers required little operator attention during the interim. An MPAA investigator downloaded between five and ten DVD-sourced movies over the Internet after December 1999. At least one web site contains a list of 650 motion pictures, said to have been decrypted and compressed with DivX, that purportedly are available for sale, trade, or free download. And although the Court does not accept the list, which is hearsay, as proof of the truth of the matters asserted therein, it does note that advertisements for decrypted versions of copyrighted movies first appeared on the Internet in substantial numbers in late 1999, following the posting of DeCSS.

The net of all this is reasonably plain. DeCSS is a free, effective, and fast means of decrypting plaintiffs' DVDs and copying them to computer hard drives. DivX, which is available over the Internet for nothing, with the investment of some time and effort, permits compression of the decrypted files to sizes that readily fit on a writeable CD-ROM. Copies of such CD-ROMs can be produced very cheaply and distributed as easily as other pirated intellectual property. While not everyone with Internet access now will find it convenient to send or receive DivX'd copies of pirated motion pictures over the Internet, the availability of high speed network connections in many businesses and institutions, and their growing availability in homes, make Internet and other network traffic in pirated copies a growing threat.

These circumstances have two major implications for plaintiffs. First, the availability of DeCSS on the Internet effectively has compromised plaintiffs' system of copyright protection for DVDs, requiring them either to tolerate increased piracy or to expend resources to develop and implement a replacement system unless the availability of DeCSS is terminated. It is analogous to the publication of a bank vault combination in a national newspaper. Even if no one uses the combination to open the vault, its mere publication has the effect of defeating the bank's security system, forcing the bank to reprogram the lock. Development and implementation of a new DVD copy protection system, however, is far more difficult and costly than reprogramming a combination lock and may carry with it the added problem of rendering the existing installed base of compliant DVD players obsolete.

Second, the application of DeCSS to copy and distribute motion pictures on DVD, both on CD-ROMs and via the Internet, threatens to reduce the studios' revenue from the sale and rental of DVDs. It threatens also to impede new, potentially lucrative initiatives for the distribution of motion pictures in digital form, such as video-on-demand via the Internet.

In consequence, plaintiffs already have been gravely injured. As the pressure for and competition to supply more and more users with faster and faster network connections grows, the injury will multiply.

. . .

C. Linking to Sites Offering DeCSS

Plaintiffs seek also to enjoin defendants from "linking" their 2600.com web site to other sites that make DeCSS available to users. Their request obviously stems in no small part from what defendants themselves have termed their act of "electronic civil disobedience"—their attempt to defeat the purpose of the preliminary injunction by (a) offering the practical equivalent of making DeCSS available on their own web site by electronically linking users to other sites still offering DeCSS, and (b) encouraging other sites that had not been enjoined to offer the program. The dispositive question is whether linking to another web site containing DeCSS constitutes "offering [DeCSS] to the public" or "providing or otherwise trafficking" in it within the meaning of the DMCA. Answering this question requires careful consideration of the nature and types of linking.

Most web pages are written in computer languages, chiefly HTML, which allow the programmer to prescribe the appearance of the web page on the computer screen and, in addition, to instruct the computer to perform an operation if the cursor is placed over a particular point on the screen and the mouse then clicked. Programming a particular point on a screen to transfer the user to another web page when the point, referred to as a hyperlink, is clicked is called linking. Web pages can be designed to link to other web pages on the same site or to web pages maintained by different sites.

As noted earlier, the links that defendants established on their web site are of several types. Some transfer the user to a web page on an outside site that contains a good deal of information of various types, does not itself contain a link to DeCSS, but that links, either directly or via a series of other pages, to another page on the same site that posts the software. It then is up to the user to follow the link or series of links on the linked-to web site in order to arrive at the page with the DeCSS link and commence the download of the software. Others take the user to a page on an outside web site on which there appears a direct link to the DeCSS software and which may or may not contain text or links other than the DeCSS link. The user has only to click on the DeCSS link to commence the download. Still others may directly transfer the user to a file on the linked-to web site such that the download of DeCSS to the user's computer automatically commences without further user intervention.

The statute makes it unlawful to offer, provide or otherwise traffic in described technology. To "traffic" in something is to engage in dealings in it, conduct that necessarily involves awareness of the nature of the subject of the trafficking. To "provide" something, in the sense used in the statute, is to make it available or furnish it. To "offer" is to present or hold it out for consideration. The phrase "or otherwise traffic in" modifies and gives meaning to the words "offer" and "provide." In consequence, the anti-trafficking provision of the DMCA is implicated where one presents, holds out or makes a circumvention technology or device available, knowing its nature, for the purpose of allowing others to acquire it.

To the extent that defendants have linked to sites that automatically commence the process of downloading DeCSS upon a user being transferred by defendants' hyperlinks, there can be no serious question. Defendants are engaged in the functional equivalent of transferring the DeCSS code to the user themselves.

Substantially the same is true of defendants' hyperlinks to web pages that display nothing more than the DeCSS code or present the user only with the choice of commencing a download of DeCSS and no other content. The only distinction is that the entity extending to the user the option of downloading the program is the transferee site rather than defendants, a distinction without a difference.

Potentially more troublesome might be links to pages that offer a good deal of content other than DeCSS but that offer a hyperlink for downloading, or transferring to a page for downloading, DeCSS. If one assumed, for the purposes of argument, that the *Los Angeles Times* web site somewhere contained the DeCSS code, it would be wrong to say that anyone who linked to the *Los Angeles Times* web site, regardless of purpose or the manner in which the link was described, thereby offered, provided or otherwise trafficked in DeCSS merely because DeCSS happened to be available on a site to which one linked. But that is not this case. Defendants urged others to post DeCSS in an effort to disseminate DeCSS and to inform defendants that they were doing so. Defendants then linked their site to those "mirror" sites, after first checking to ensure that the mirror sites in fact were posting DeCSS or something that looked like it, and proclaimed on their own site that DeCSS could be had by clicking on the hyperlinks on defendants' site. By doing so, they offered, provided or otherwise trafficked in DeCSS, and they continue to do so to this day.

. . .

C. Linking

As indicated above, the DMCA reaches links deliberately created by a web site operator for the purpose of disseminating technology that enables the user to circumvent access controls on copyrighted works. The question is whether it may do so consistent with the First Amendment.

Links bear a relationship to the information superhighway comparable to the relationship that roadway signs bear to roads but they are more functional. Like roadway signs, they point out the direction. Unlike roadway signs, they take one almost instantaneously to the desired destination with the mere click of an electronic mouse. Thus, like computer code in general, they have both expressive and functional elements. Also like computer code, they are within the area of First Amendment concern. Hence, the constitutionality of the DMCA as applied to defendants' linking is determined by the same *O'Brien* standard that governs trafficking in the circumvention technology generally.

There is little question that the application of the DMCA to the linking at issue in this case would serve, at least to some extent, the same substantial governmental interest as its application to defendants' posting of the DeCSS code. Defendants' posting and their linking amount to very much the same thing. Similarly, the regulation of the linking at issue here is "unrelated to the suppression of free expression" for the same reason as the regulation of the posting. The third prong of the *O'Brien* test as subsequently interpreted—whether the "regulation promotes a substantial government interest that would be achieved less effectively absent the regulation"—is a somewhat closer call.

Defendants and, by logical extension, others may be enjoined from posting DeCSS. Plaintiffs may seek legal redress against anyone who persists in posting notwithstanding this decision. Hence, barring defendants from linking to sites against which plaintiffs readily may take legal action would advance the statutory purpose of preventing dissemination of circumvention technology, but it would do so less effectively than would actions by plaintiffs directly against the sites that post. For precisely this reason, however, the real significance of an anti-linking injunction would not be with U.S. web sites subject to the DMCA, but with foreign sites that arguably are not subject to it and not subject to suit here. An anti-linking injunction to that extent would have a significant impact and thus materially advance a substantial governmental purpose. In consequence, the Court concludes that an injunction against linking to other sites posting DeCSS satisfies the *O'Brien* standard. There remains, however, one further important point.

Links are "what unify the [World Wide] Web into a single body of knowledge, and what makes the Web unique." *ACLU v. Reno, 929 F. Supp. 824, 837 (E.D. Pa. 1996).* They "are the mainstay of the Internet and indispensable to its convenient access to the vast world of information." Richard Raysman & Peter Brown, p. 3, col. 1. They often are used in ways that do a great deal to promote the free exchange of ideas and information that is a central value of our nation. Anything that would impose strict liability on a web site operator for the entire contents of any web site to which the operator linked therefore would raise grave constitutional concerns, as web site operators would be inhibited from linking for fear of exposure to liability. And it is equally clear that exposing those who use links to liability under the DMCA might chill their use, as some web site operators confronted with claims that they have posted circumvention technology falling within the statute may be more inclined to remove the allegedly offending link rather than test the issue in court. Moreover, web sites often contain a great variety of things, and a ban on linking to a site that contains DeCSS amidst other content threatens to restrict communication of this information to an excessive degree.

The possible chilling effect of a rule permitting liability for or injunctions against Internet hyperlinks is a genuine concern. But it is not unique to the issue of linking. The constitutional law of defamation provides a highly relevant analogy. The threat of defamation suits creates the same risk of self-censorship, the same chilling effect, for the traditional press as a prohibition of linking to sites containing circumvention technology poses for web site operators. Just as the potential chilling effect of defamation suits has not utterly immunized the press from all actions for defamation, however, the potential chilling effect of DMCA liability cannot utterly immunize web site operators from all actions for disseminating circumvention technology. And the solution to the problem is the same: The adoption of a standard of culpability sufficiently high to immunize the activity, whether it is publishing a newspaper or linking, except in cases in which the conduct in question has little or no redeeming constitutional value.

In the defamation area, this has been accomplished by a two-tiered constitutional standard. There may be no liability under the First Amendment for defamation of a public official or a public figure unless the plaintiff proves, by clear and convincing evidence, that the defendant published the offending statement with knowledge of its falsity or with serious doubt as to its truth. Liability in private figure cases, on the other hand, may not be imposed absent proof at least of negligence under *Gertz v. Robert Welch, Inc.* A similar approach would minimize any chilling effect here.

The other concern—that a liability based on a link to another site simply because the other site happened to contain DeCSS or some other circumvention technology in the midst of other perfectly appropriate content could be overkill—also is readily dealt with. The offense under the DMCA is offering, providing or otherwise trafficking in circumvention technology. An essential ingredient, as explained above, is a desire to bring about the dissemination. Hence, a strong requirement of that forbidden purpose is an essential prerequisite to any liability for linking.

Accordingly, there may be no injunction against, nor liability for, linking to a site containing circumvention technology, the offering of which is unlawful under the DMCA, absent clear and convincing evidence that those responsible for the link (a) know at the relevant time that the offending material is on the linked-to site, (b) know that it is circumvention technology that may not lawfully be offered, and (c) create or maintain the link for the purpose of disseminating that technology. Such a standard will limit the fear of liability on the part of web site operators just as the *New York Times* standard gives the press great comfort in publishing all sorts of material that would have been actionable at common law, even in the face of flat denials by the subjects of their stories. And it will not subject web site operators to liability for linking to a site containing proscribed technology where the link exists for purposes other than dissemination of that technology.

In this case, plaintiffs have established by clear and convincing evidence that these defendants linked to sites posting DeCSS, knowing that it was a circumvention device. Indeed, they initially touted it as a way to get free movies, and they later maintained the links to promote the dissemination of the program in an effort to defeat effective judicial relief. They now know that dissemination of DeCSS violates the DMCA. An anti-linking injunction on these facts does no violence to the First Amendment. Nor should it chill the activities of web site operators dealing with different materials, as they may be held liable only on a compelling showing of deliberate evasion of the statute.

IV. Relief

A. Injury to Plaintiffs

The DMCA provides that "any person injured by a violation of section 1201 or 1202 may bring a civil action in an appropriate United States court for such violation." *17 U.S.C. § 1203(a)*. For the reasons set forth above, plaintiffs obviously have suffered and, absent effective relief, will continue to suffer injury by virtue of the ready availability of means of circumventing the CSS access control system on their DVDs. Defendants nevertheless argue that they have not met the injury requirement of the statute. Their contentions are a farrago of distortions.

They begin with the assertion that plaintiffs have failed to prove that decrypted motion pictures actually are available. To be sure, plaintiffs might have done a better job of proving what appears to be reasonably obvious. They certainly could have followed up on more of the 650 movie titles listed on the web site described above to establish that the titles in fact were available. But the evidence they did adduce is not nearly as meager as defendants would have it. Dr. Shamos did pursue and obtain a pirated copy of a copyrighted, DivX'd motion picture from someone he met in an Internet chat room. An MPAA investigator downloaded between five and ten such copies. And the sudden appearance of listings of available motion pictures on the Internet promptly after DeCSS became available is far from lacking in evidentiary significance. In any case, in order to obtain the relief sought here, plaintiffs need show only a threat of injury by reason of a violation of the statute. The Court finds that plaintiffs overwhelmingly have established a clear threat of injury by reason of defendants' violation of the statute.

Defendants next maintain that plaintiffs exaggerate the extent of the threatened injury. They claim that the studios in fact believe that DeCSS is not a threat. But the only basis for that contention is a couple of quotations from statements that the MPAA or one or another studio made (or considered making but did not in fact issue) to the effect that it was not concerned about DeCSS or that it was inconvenient to use. These statements, however, were attempts to "spin" public opinion. They do not now reflect the actual state of affairs or the studios' actual views, if they ever did.

Third, defendants contend that there is no evidence that any decrypted movies that may be available, if any there are, were decrypted with DeCSS. They maintain that "many utilities and devices . . . can decrypt DVDs equally well and often faster and with greater ease than by using DeCSS." This is a substantial exaggeration. There appear to be a few other so-called rippers, but the Court finds that DeCSS is usable on a broader range of DVDs than any of the others. Further, there is no credible evidence that any other utility is faster or easier to use than DeCSS. Indeed, the Court concludes that DeCSS is the superior product, as evidenced by the fact that the web site promoting DivX as a tool for obtaining usable copies of copyrighted movies recommends the use of DeCSS, rather than anything else, for the decryption step and that the apparent availability of pirated motion pictures shot up so dramatically upon the introduction of DeCSS.

B. Permanent Injunction and Declaratory Relief

Plaintiffs seek a permanent injunction barring defendants from posting DeCSS on their web site and from linking their site to others that make DeCSS available.

The starting point, as always, is the statute. The DMCA provides in relevant part that the court in an action brought pursuant to its terms "may grant temporary and permanent injunctions on such terms as it deems reasonable to prevent or restrain a violation. . . ." *17 U.S.C. § 1203(b)(1).* Where statutes in substance so provide, injunctive relief is appropriate if there is a reasonable likelihood of future violations absent such relief and, in cases brought by private plaintiffs, if the plaintiff lacks an adequate remedy at law.

In this case, it is quite likely that defendants, unless enjoined, will continue to violate the Act. Defendants are in the business of disseminating information to assist hackers in "cracking" various types of technological security systems. And while defendants argue that they promptly stopped posting DeCSS when enjoined preliminarily from doing so, thus allegedly demonstrating their willingness to comply with the law, their reaction to the preliminary injunction in fact cuts the other way. Upon being enjoined from posting DeCSS themselves, defendants encouraged others to "mirror" the information—that is, to post DeCSS—and linked their own web site to mirror sites in order to assist users of defendants' web site in obtaining DeCSS despite the injunction barring defendants from providing it directly. While there is no claim that this activity violated the letter of the preliminary injunction, and it therefore presumably was not contumacious, and while its status under the DMCA was somewhat uncertain, it was a studied effort to defeat the purpose of the preliminary injunction. In consequence, the Court finds that there is a substantial likelihood of future violations absent injunctive relief.

There also is little doubt that plaintiffs have no adequate remedy at law. The only potential legal remedy would be an action for damages under Section

1203(c), which provides for recovery of actual damages or, upon the election of the plaintiff, statutory damages of up to $2,500 per offer of DeCSS. Proof of actual damages in a case of this nature would be difficult if not virtually impossible, as it would involve proof of the extent to which motion picture attendance, sales of broadcast and other motion picture rights, and sales and rentals of DVDs and video tapes of movies were and will be impacted by the availability of DVD decryption technology. Difficulties in determining what constitutes an "offer" of DeCSS in a world in which the code is available to much of the world via Internet postings, among other problems, render statutory damages an inadequate means of redressing plaintiffs' claimed injuries. Indeed, difficulties such as this have led to the presumption that copyright and trademark infringement cause irreparable injury, i.e., injury for which damages are not an adequate remedy. The Court therefore holds that the traditional requirements for issuance of a permanent injunction have been satisfied. Yet there remains another point for consideration.

Defendants argue that an injunction in this case would be futile because DeCSS already is all over the Internet. They say an injunction would be comparable to locking the barn door after the horse is gone. And the Court has been troubled by that possibility. But the countervailing arguments overcome that concern.

To begin with, any such conclusion effectively would create all the wrong incentives by allowing defendants to continue violating the DMCA simply because others, many doubtless at defendants' urging, are doing so as well. Were that the law, defendants confronted with the possibility of injunctive relief would be well advised to ensure that others engage in the same unlawful conduct in order to set up the argument that an injunction against the defendants would be futile because everyone else is doing the same thing.

Second, and closely related, is the fact that this Court is sorely "troubled by the notion that any Internet user . . . can destroy valuable intellectual property rights by posting them over the Internet." *Religious Tech. Ctr. v. Netcom Online Comm. Serv., Inc., 923 F. Supp. 1231, 1256 (N.D. Cal. 1995).* While equity surely should not act where the controversy has become moot, it ought to look very skeptically at claims that the defendant or others already have done all the harm that might be done before the injunction issues.

The key to reconciling these views is that the focus of injunctive relief is on the defendants before the Court. If a plaintiff seeks to enjoin a defendant from burning a pasture, it is no answer that there is a wild fire burning in its direction. If the defendant itself threatens the plaintiff with irreparable harm, then equity will enjoin the defendant from carrying out the threat even if other threats abound and even if part of the pasture already is burned.

These defendants would harm plaintiffs every day on which they post DeCSS on their heavily trafficked web site and link to other sites that post it because someone who does not have DeCSS thereby might obtain it. They thus threaten plaintiffs with immediate and irreparable injury. They will not be allowed to continue to do so simply because others may do so as well. In short, this Court, like others than have faced the issued, is "not persuaded that modern technology has withered the strong right arm of equity." *Com-Share, Inc. v. Computer Complex, Inc., 338 F. Supp. 1229, 1239 (E.D. Mich. 1971).* Indeed, the likelihood is that this decision will serve notice on others that "the strong right arm of equity" may be brought to bear against them absent a change in their conduct and thus contribute to a climate of appropriate respect for intellectual property rights in an age in which the excitement of ready access to untold quantities of information has blurred in some minds the fact that taking what is not yours and not freely offered to you is stealing. Appropriate injunctive and declaratory relief will issue simultaneously with this opinion.

V. Miscellaneous Contentions

There remain for consideration two other matters, plaintiffs' application for costs and attorney's fees and defendants' pretrial complaints concerning discovery.

The DMCA permits awards of costs and attorney's fees to the prevailing party in the discretion of the Court. Insofar as attorney's fees are concerned, this is an exception to the so-called "American rule" pursuant to which each side in a litigation customarily bears its own attorney's fees. As this was a test case raising important issues, it would be inappropriate to award attorney's fees pursuant to the DMCA. There is no comparable reason, however, for failing to award costs, particularly as taxable costs are related to the excessive dis-covery demands that the Court already has commented upon.

A final word is in order in view of defendants' repeated pretrial claims that their discovery efforts were being thwarted. During the course of the trial, they applied for leave to take one deposition, which was granted. At no point did they make any showing that they were hampered in presenting their case or meeting the plaintiffs' case by virtue of any failure to obtain discovery. They applied for no continuance. They have not sought a new trial. And though they estimated that their case would take several weeks to present, the entire trial was completed in six days. Indeed, in the Court's view, the trial fully vindicated its pretrial assessment that there were, in actuality, very few genuinely disputed questions of material fact, and most of those involved expert testimony that was readily available to both sides. Examination of the trial record will reveal that virtually the entire case could have been stipulated, although the legal conclusions to be drawn from the stipulated facts of course would have remained a matter of controversy.

VI. Conclusion

In the final analysis, the dispute between these parties is simply put if not necessarily simply resolved.

Plaintiffs have invested huge sums over the years in producing motion pictures in reliance upon a legal framework that, through the law of copyright, has ensured that they will have the exclusive right to copy and distribute those motion pictures for economic gain. They contend that the advent of new technology should not alter this long established structure.

Defendants, on the other hand, are adherents of a movement that believes that information should be available without charge to anyone clever enough to break into the computer systems or data storage media in which it is located. Less radically, they have raised a legitimate concern about the possible impact on traditional fair use of access control measures in the digital era.

Each side is entitled to its views. In our society, however, clashes of competing interests like this are resolved by Congress. For now, at least, Congress has resolved this clash in the DMCA and in plaintiffs' favor. Given the peculiar characteristics of computer programs for circumventing encryption and other access control measures, the DMCA as applied to posting and linking here does not contravene the First Amendment. Accordingly, plaintiffs are entitled to appropriate injunctive and declaratory relief.

So Ordered.

Appendix D

People for the Ethical Treatment of Animals, Inc., Plaintiff, v. Michael T. Doughney, Defendant

113 F. Supp. 2d 915 (E.D. Virginia, 2000)

Memorandum Opinion

...This lawsuit arose from a dispute between Plaintiff, People for the Ethical Treatment of Animals ("PETA"), and Defendant, Michael Doughney ("Doughney"), regarding the use of the internet domain name "PETA.ORG." PETA is a non-profit, charitable corporation established in August 1980. PETA has affiliated animal protection organizations in the United Kingdom, Germany, the Netherlands, and India who all operate under the name PETA. On August 4, 1992, PETA was given U.S. Trademark Registration Number 1,705,510 duly issued by the United States Patent and Trademark Office for the service mark "PETA" for "educational services; namely providing programs and seminars on the subject of animal rights welfare," and, "promoting the public awareness of the need to prevent cruelty and mistreatment of animals." PETA has used the PETA trademark and trade name continuously in interstate commerce and foreign commerce since 1980.

Defendant, Michael Doughney ("Doughney"), registered many domain names in September 1995, including "PETA.ORG." At that time, PETA had no web sites of its own. Doughney registered "PETA.ORG" with Network Solutions, Inc. for "People Eating Tasty Animals" which he represented to Network Solutions, Inc. was a non-profit organization. No such organization was in existence at the time of the registration of the web site or since that time. Doughney also represented to Network Solutions, Inc. that the name "PETA. ORG" "does not interfere with or infringe upon the rights of any third party."

Doughney's "PETA.ORG" web site contained information and materials antithetical to PETA's purpose. When in operation, "www.peta.org" contained the following description of the web site: "A resource for those who enjoy eating meat, wearing fur and leather, hunting, and the fruits of scientific research." There were over thirty links on the web site to commercial sites promoting among other things the sale of leather goods and meats. Until an Internet user actually reached the "PETA.ORG" web site, where the screen read "People Eating Tasty Animals," the user had no way of knowing that the "PETA.ORG" web site was not owned, sponsored or endorsed by PETA.

On January 29, 1996, PETA sent Doughney a letter requesting that he relinquish his registration of the "PETA.ORG" name because "it uses and infringes upon the longstanding registered service mark of People for the Ethical Treatment of Animals, whose service mark 'PETA' currently is in full force and effect."

PETA then complained to Network Solutions, Inc. and on or about May 2, 1996, Network Solutions, Inc. placed the "PETA.ORG" domain name on "hold" status. Pursuant to Network Solutions, Inc.'s "hold" status designation, the "PETA.ORG" domain name may not be used by any person or entity. After "PETA.ORG" was put on "hold" status, Doughney transferred the contents of that web site to the internet address "www.mtd.com/tasty."

PETA brought this suit alleging claims for service mark infringement in violation of *15 U.S.C. § 1114* (Count I), unfair competition in violation of *15 U.S.C. § 1125* (a) and Virginia common law (Counts II and VI), service mark dilution and cybersquatting in violation of *15 U.S.C. § 1125* (c) (Count VII). PETA has voluntarily withdrawn Counts III, IV and V of its Amended Complaint. Doughney claims there is no infringement because its web site is a parody. PETA has dropped its claim for damages and seeks the following equitable relief: to enjoin Doughney's unauthorized use of its registered service mark "PETA" in the internet domain name "PETA.ORG," to force Doughney's assignment of the "PETA.ORG" domain name to PETA.

To make out a case for service or trade mark infringement and/or unfair competition, a Plaintiff must prove the following elements: (1) that Plaintiff possesses a Mark; (2) that Defendant uses the Plaintiff's Mark; (3) that such use occurs in commerce; (4) in connection with the sale or offering for sale, distribution, or advertising of goods or services; and (5) in a way that is likely to cause confusion among consumers. *15 U.S.C. § § 1114,* 1125(a).

First, PETA owns the PETA Mark and Defendant admits the PETA Mark's validity and incontestability. The PETA Mark is thus presumed to be distinctive as a matter of law. Second, Doughney used the identical PETA Mark to register "PETA.ORG" and posting a web site at the Internet address "www.peta.org." Third, Doughney admits that his use of the PETA Mark was "in commerce."

The fourth element requires that Defendant's use of the PETA Mark be made in connection with the sale, distribution, or advertising of goods or services. This does not require that Defendant actually caused goods or services to be placed into the stream of commerce. The term "services" has been interpreted broadly to include the dissemination of information, including purely ideological information. Defendant's use of the PETA Mark was "in connection" with goods and services because the use of a misleading domain name has been found to be "in connection with the distribution of services" when it impacts on the Plaintiff's business: It is likely to prevent Internet users from reaching [PETA]'s own Internet web site. The prospective users of [PETA]'s services who mistakenly access Defendant's web site may fail to continue to search for [PETA]'s own home page, due to anger, frustration, or the belief that the Plaintiff's home page does not exist.

In addition, the "PETA.ORG" web site contained over thirty separate hyperlinks to commercial operations offering goods and services, including fur, leather, magazines, clothing, equipment and guide services. Under the law, even one such link is sufficient to establish the commercial use requirement of the Lanham Act.

Last, Defendant's use of PETA's Mark did cause confusion. Doughney copied the Mark identically. This creates a presumption of likelihood of confusion among internet users as a matter of law. In addition, there was evidence of actual confusion by those using the internet who were trying to locate PETA and instead found Doughney's web site.

Doughney's web site certainly dilutes the Mark of PETA. To win on summary judgment for a claim for dilution under *15 U.S.C. § 1125* (c)(1), Plaintiff must show that the undisputed facts demonstrate that Defendant's use of "PETA.ORG" diluted the PETA Mark's distinctive quality. Dilution is "the lessening of the capacity of a famous mark to identify and distinguish goods or services, regardless of the presence or absence of (1) competition between the owner of the famous mark and other parties, or (2) likelihood of confusion, mistake or deception." *15 U.S.C. § 1127.* Dilution can occur by "tarnishment" or "blurring." *Jews for Jesus, 993 F. Supp. at 305; Ringling Bros., 170 F.3d at 452.*

Defendant is guilty of "blurring" the famous PETA Mark because (1) Defendant used the identical PETA Mark to mentally associate PETA.ORG to the PETA Mark; and (2) such use caused; (3) actual economic harm to the PETA Mark by lessening its selling power as an advertising agent for PETA's goods and services. Doughney's site included materials antithetical to the purpose and message of PETA in that "PETA.ORG" included links to commercial enterprises engaged in conduct directly contrary to PETA's animal protection efforts.

PETA is also entitled to Summary Judgment under the Anticybersquatting Consumer Protection Act ("ACPA"), *15 U.S.C. § 1125* (d)(1)(A). To succeed on Summary Judgment, Plaintiff must show that Defendant (1) has a bad-faith intent to profit from using "PETA.ORG" and (2) the "PETA.ORG" domain name is identical or confusingly similar to, or dilutive of, the distinctive and famous PETA Mark *15 U.S.C. § 1125* (d)(1)(A). The second element has been proved for reasons stated above. As to the first element, under the ACPA, there are nine factors a court must consider in making a determination of whether the Defendant had a bad faith intent. *15 U.S.C. § 1125* (d)(1)(B). Applying these factors, it appears that Doughney had the requisite bad faith intent.

First, Defendant possessed no intellectual property rights in "PETA.ORG" when he registered the domain name in 1995. Second, the "PETA.ORG" domain name is not the Defendant, Michael T. Doughney's legal name or any name that is otherwise used to identify the Defendant. Third, Defendant had not engaged in prior use of the "PETA.ORG" domain name in connection with the bona fide offering of any goods or services prior to registering "PETA.ORG." Fourth, Defendant used the PETA Mark in a commercial manner. Fifth, Defendant clearly intended to confuse, mislead and divert internet users into accessing his web site which contained information antithetical and therefore harmful to the goodwill represented by the PETA Mark. Sixth, on Doughney's "PETA.ORG" web site, Doughney made reference to seeing what PETA would offer him if PETA did not like his web site. Seventh, Defendant, when registering the domain name "PETA.ORG," falsely stated that "People Eating Tasty Animals" was a non-profit educational organization and that this web site did not infringe any trademark. Eighth, Defendant has registered other Internet domain names which are identical or similar to either marks or names of famous people or organizations he opposes. Ninth, the PETA Mark used in the "PETA.ORG" domain name is distinctive and famous and was so at the time. Defendant registered this site in September 1995.

Doughney contends there is no infringement in that his web site was a parody. A parody exists when two antithetical ideas appear at the same time. In this instance, an internet user would not realize that they were not on an official PETA web site until after they had used PETA's Mark to access the web page "www.peta.org." Only then would they find Doughney's People Eating Tasty Animals. Doughney knew he was causing confusion by use of the Mark and admitted that it was "possible" that some Internet users would be confused when they activated "PETA.ORG" and found the "People Eating Tasty Animals" web site. He also admitted that "many people" would initially assume that they were accessing an authentic PETA web site at "www.peta.org." Only after arriving at the "PETA.ORG" web site could the web site browser determine that this was not a web site owned, controlled or sponsored by PETA. Therefore, the two images: (1) the famous PETA name and (2) the "People Eating Tasty Animals" web site was not a parody because not simultaneous.

The Defendant's affirmative defense of trademark misuse is inapplicable. In 1998, PETA registered the domain names "ringlingbrothers.com," "voguemagazine.com," and "pg.info." Each web site contained messages from PETA criticizing Ringling Bros.-Barnum & Bailey Combined, Vogue Magazine, and Procter & Gamble Company for mistreatment of animals. In each instance, "ringlingbrothers," "voguemagazine" and "pginfo" were not and are not registered trademarks. PETA received complaints from Conde Nast Publications that owns Vogue Magazine and from the Ringling Bros.-Barnum & Bailey Combined Shows regarding PETA's web sites bearing their names. In each case, PETA voluntarily and immediately assigned the domain names to the complaining party. At no time did PETA receive any correspondence of any kind from Procter & Gamble Company complaining about PETA's registration and use of the internet domain name "pginfo.net." Doughney had no relation to any of these web sites and suffered no damages from PETA's operation of any of these web sites.

Defendant's affirmative defense is based in part on a constitutional argument. Doughney contends that this case is an attempt to quash his First Amendment rights to express disagreement with their organization. PETA does not seek to keep Doughney from criticizing PETA. They ask that Doughney not use their mark. When Network Solutions, Inc. placed "PETA.ORG" on "hold" status, Doughney transferred the entire web page to one of his other internet sites, "mtd.com/tasty." PETA has not complained about that web site and even concedes that Doughney has a right to criticize PETA or any organization.

The proposed rule would foreclose judicial relief anywhere because joinder of all plainly would be impossible in any one place, and technology does not permit identification of which wrongdoer's posting or product led to which pirated copy of a copyrighted work.

Defendant also raises as his trademark misuse affirmative defense an "unclean hands" argument. However, the doctrine of unclean hands applies only with respect to the right in suit. What is material is not that the plaintiff's hands are dirty, but that he dirtied them in acquiring the right he now asserts. The purported grounds for Defendant's "unclean hands"—i.e. PETA's disputes with Ringling Bros. and Vogue, and PETA's web site that is critical of Proctor & Gamble—are not at issue in this suit and thus, are not properly the subject of an unclean hands defense.

As PETA has proven its case for its infringement and dilution claims and Doughney can offer no viable defenses to PETA's claims, Summary Judgment should be granted in favor of PETA.

An appropriate Order shall issue.

Appendix E

Statutes

Digital Millennium Copyright Act, 17 USC § 1201 (2000)

§ 1201. Circumvention of copyright protection systems

(a) Violations regarding circumvention of technological measures.

(1) (A) No person shall circumvent a technological measure that effectively controls access to a work protected under this title. The prohibition contained in the preceding sentence shall take effect at the end of the 2-year period beginning on the date of the enactment of this chapter [enacted Oct. 28, 1998].

(B) The prohibition contained in subparagraph (A) shall not apply to persons who are users of a copyrighted work which is in a particular class of works, if such persons are, or are likely to be in the succeeding 3-year period, adversely affected by virtue of such prohibition in their ability to make noninfringing uses of that particular class of works under this title, as determined under subparagraph (C).

(C) During the 2-year period described in subparagraph (A), and during each succeeding 3-year period, the Librarian of Congress, upon the recommendation of the Register of Copyrights, who shall consult with the Assistant Secretary for Communications and Information of the Department of Commerce and report and comment on his or her views in making such recommendation, shall make the determination in a rulemaking proceeding for purposes of subparagraph (B) of whether persons who are users of a copyrighted work are, or are likely to be in the succeeding 3-year period, adversely affected by the prohibition under subparagraph (A) in their ability to make noninfringing uses under this title of a particular class of copyrighted works. In conducting such rulemaking, the Librarian shall examine—

(i) the availability for use of copyrighted works;

(ii) the availability for use of works for nonprofit archival, preservation, and educational purposes;

(iii) the impact that the prohibition on the circumvention of technological measures applied to copyrighted works has on criticism, comment, news reporting, teaching, scholarship, or research;

(iv) the effect of circumvention of technological measures on the market for or value of copyrighted works; and

(v) such other factors as the Librarian considers appropriate.

(D) The Librarian shall publish any class of copyrighted works for which the Librarian has determined, pursuant to the rulemaking conducted under subparagraph (C), that noninfringing uses by persons who are users of a copyrighted work are, or are likely to be, adversely affected, and the prohibition contained in subparagraph (A) shall not apply to such users with respect to such class of works for the ensuing 3-year period.

(E) Neither the exception under subparagraph (B) from the applicability of the prohibition contained in subparagraph (A), nor any determination made in a rulemaking conducted under subparagraph (C), may be used as a defense in any action to enforce any provision of this title other than this paragraph.

(2) No person shall manufacture, import, offer to the public, provide, or otherwise traffic in any technology, product, service, device, component, or part thereof, that—

(A) is primarily designed or produced for the purpose of circumventing a technological measure that effectively controls access to a work protected under this title;

(B) has only limited commercially significant purpose or use other than to circumvent a technological measure that effectively controls access to a work protected under this title; or

(C) is marketed by that person or another acting in concert with that person with that person's knowledge for use in circumventing a technological measure that effectively controls access to a work protected under this title.

(3) As used in this subsection—

(A) to "circumvent a technological measure" means to descramble a scrambled work, to decrypt an encrypted work, or otherwise to avoid, bypass, remove, deactivate, or impair a technological measure, without the authority of the copyright owner; and

(B) a technological measure "effectively controls access to a work" if the measure, in the ordinary course of its operation, requires the application of information, or a process or a treatment, with the authority of the copyright owner, to gain access to the work.

(b) Additional violations.

(1) No person shall manufacture, import, offer to the public, provide, or otherwise traffic in any technology, product, service, device, component, or part thereof, that—

(A) is primarily designed or produced for the purpose of circumventing protection afforded by a technological measure that effectively protects a right of a copyright owner under this title in a work or a portion thereof;

(B) has only limited commercially significant purpose or use other than to circumvent protection afforded by a technological measure that effectively protects a right of a copyright owner under this title in a work or a portion thereof; or

(C) is marketed by that person or another acting in concert with that person with that person's knowledge for use in circumventing protection afforded by a technological measure that effectively protects a right of a copyright owner under this title in a work or a portion thereof.

(2) As used in this subsection—

(A) to "circumvent protection afforded by a technological measure" means avoiding, bypassing, removing, deactivating, or otherwise impairing a technological measure; and

(B) a technological measure "effectively protects a right of a copyright owner under this title" if the measure, in the ordinary course of its operation, prevents, restricts, or otherwise limits the exercise of a right of a copyright owner under this title.

(c) Other rights, etc., not affected.

(1) Nothing in this section shall affect rights, remedies, limitations, or defenses to copyright infringement, including fair use, under this title.

(2) Nothing in this section shall enlarge or diminish vicarious or contrib.-utory liability for copyright infringement in connection with any technology, product, service, device, component, or part thereof.

(3) Nothing in this section shall require that the design of, or design and selection of parts and components for, a consumer electronics, telecommunications, or computing product provide for a response to any particular technological measure, so long as such part or component, or the product in which such part or component is integrated, does not otherwise fall within the prohibitions of subsection (a)(2) or (b)(1).

(4) Nothing in this section shall enlarge or diminish any rights of free speech or the press for activities using consumer electronics, telecommunications, or computing products.

(d) Exemption for nonprofit libraries, archives, and educational institutions.

(1) A nonprofit library, archives, or educational institution which gains access to a commercially exploited copyrighted work solely in order to make a good faith determination of whether to acquire a copy of that work for the sole purpose of engaging in conduct permitted under this title shall not be in violation of subsection (a)(1)(A). A copy of a work to which access has been gained under this paragraph—

(A) may not be retained longer than necessary to make such good faith determination; and

(B) may not be used for any other purpose.

(2) The exemption made available under paragraph (1) shall only apply with respect to a work when an identical copy of that work is not reasonably available in another form.

(3) A nonprofit library, archives, or educational institution that willfully for the purpose of commercial advantage or financial gain violates paragraph (1)—

(A) shall, for the first offense, be subject to the civil remedies under section 1203; and

(B) shall, for repeated or subsequent offenses, in addition to the civil remedies under section 1203, forfeit the exemption provided under paragraph (1).

(4) This subsection may not be used as a defense to a claim under subsection (a)(2) or (b), nor may this subsection permit a nonprofit library, archives, or educational institution to manufacture, import, offer to the public, provide, or otherwise traffic in any technology, product, service, component, or part thereof, which circumvents a technological measure.

(5) In order for a library or archives to qualify for the exemption under this subsection, the collections of that library or archives shall be—

(A) open to the public; or

(B) available not only to researchers affiliated with the library or archives or with the institution of which it is a part, but also to other persons doing research in a specialized field.

(e) Law enforcement, intelligence, and other government activities. This section does not prohibit any lawfully authorized investigative, protective, information security, or intelligence activity of an officer, agent, or employee of the United States, a State, or a political subdivision of a State, or a person acting pursuant to a contract with the United States, a State, or a political subdivision of a State. For purposes of this subsection, the term "information security" means activities carried out in order to identify and address the vulnerabilities of a government computer, computer system, or computer network.

(f) Reverse engineering.

(1) Notwithstanding the provisions of subsection (a)(1)(A), a person who has lawfully obtained the right to use a copy of a computer program may circumvent a technological measure that effectively controls access to a particular portion of that program for the sole purpose of identifying and analyzing those elements of the program that are necessary to achieve interoperability of an independently created computer program with other programs, and that have not previously been readily available to the person engaging in the circumvention, to the extent any such acts of identification and analysis do not constitute infringement under this title.

(2) Notwithstanding the provisions of subsections (a)(2) and (b), a person may develop and employ technological means to circumvent a technological measure, or to circumvent protection afforded by a technological measure, in order to enable the identification and analysis under paragraph (1), or for the purpose of enabling interoperability of an independently created computer program with other programs, if such means are necessary to achieve such interoperability, to the extent that doing so does not constitute infringement under this title.

(3) The information acquired through the acts permitted under paragraph (1), and the means permitted under paragraph (2), may be made available to others if the person referred to in paragraph (1) or (2), as the case may be, provides such information or means solely for the purpose of enabling interoperability of an independently created computer program with other programs, and to the extent that doing so does not constitute infringement under this title or violate applicable law other than this section.

(4) For purposes of this subsection, the term "interoperability" means the ability of computer programs to exchange information, and of such programs mutually to use the information which has been exchanged.

(g) Encryption research.

(1) Definitions. For purposes of this subsection—

(A) the term "encryption research" means activities necessary to identify and analyze flaws and vulnerabilities of encryption technologies applied to copyrighted works, if these activities are conducted to advance the state of knowledge in the field of encryption technology or to assist in the development of encryption products; and

(B) the term "encryption technology" means the scrambling and descrambling of information using mathematical formulas or algorithms.

(2) Permissible acts of encryption research. Notwithstanding the provisions of subsection (a)(1)(A), it is not a violation of that subsection for a person to circumvent a technological measure as applied to a copy, phonorecord, performance, or display of a published work in the course of an act of good faith encryption research if—

(A) the person lawfully obtained the encrypted copy, phonorecord, performance, or display of the published work;

(B) such act is necessary to conduct such encryption research;

(C) the person made a good faith effort to obtain authorization before the circumvention; and

(D) such act does not constitute infringement under this title or a violation of applicable law other than this section, including section 1030 of title 18 and those provisions of title 18 amended by the Computer Fraud and Abuse Act of 1986 [*18 USCS § 1030*(a)-(c), (e), (f)].

(3) Factors in determining exemption. In determining whether a person qualifies for the exemption under paragraph (2), the factors to be considered shall include—

(A) whether the information derived from the encryption research was disseminated, and if so, whether it was disseminated in a manner reasonably calculated to advance the state of knowledge or development of encryption technology, versus whether it was disseminated in a manner that facilitates infringement under this title or a violation of applicable law other than this section, including a violation of privacy or breach of security;

(B) whether the person is engaged in a legitimate course of study, is employed, or is appropriately trained or experienced, in the field of encryption technology; and

(C) whether the person provides the copyright owner of the work to which the technological measure is applied with notice of the findings and documentation of the research, and the time when such notice is provided.

(4) Use of technological means for research activities. Notwithstanding the provisions of subsection (a)(2), it is not a violation of that subsection for a person to—

(A) develop and employ technological means to circumvent a technological measure for the sole purpose of that person performing the acts of good faith encryption research described in paragraph (2); and

(B) provide the technological means to another person with whom he or she is working collaboratively for the purpose of conducting the acts of good faith encryption research described in paragraph (2) or for the purpose of having that other person verify his or her acts of good faith encryption research described in paragraph (2).

(5) Report to Congress. Not later than 1 year after the date of the enactment of this chapter [enacted Oct. 28, 1998], the Register of Copyrights and the Assistant Secretary for Communications and Information of the Department of

Commerce shall jointly report to the Congress on the effect this subsection has had on—

(A) encryption research and the development of encryption technology;

(B) the adequacy and effectiveness of technological measures designed to protect copyrighted works; and

(C) protection of copyright owners against the unauthorized access to their encrypted copyrighted works.

The report shall include legislative recommendations, if any.

(h) Exceptions regarding minors. In applying subsection (a) to a component or part, the court may consider the necessity for its intended and actual incorporation in a technology, product, service, or device, which—

(1) does not itself violate the provisions of this title; and

(2) has the sole purpose to prevent the access of minors to material on the Internet.

(i) Protection of personally identifying information.

(1) Circumvention permitted. Notwithstanding the provisions of subsection (a)(1)(A), it is not a violation of that subsection for a person to circumvent a technological measure that effectively controls access to a work protected under this title, if—

(A) the technological measure, or the work it protects, contains the capability of collecting or disseminating personally identifying information reflecting the online activities of a natural person who seeks to gain access to the work protected;

(B) in the normal course of its operation, the technological measure, or the work it protects, collects or disseminates personally identifying information about the person who seeks to gain access to the work protected, without providing conspicuous notice of such collection or dissemination to such person, and without providing such person with the capability to prevent or restrict such collection or dissemination;

(C) the act of circumvention has the sole effect of identifying and disabling the capability described in subparagraph (A), and has no other effect on the ability of any person to gain access to any work; and

(D) the act of circumvention is carried out solely for the purpose of preventing the collection or dissemination of personally identifying information about a natural person who seeks to gain access to the work protected, and is not in violation of any other law.

(2) Inapplicability to certain technological measures. This subsection does not apply to a technological measure, or a work it protects, that does not collect or disseminate personally identifying information and that is disclosed to a user as not having or using such capability.

(j) Security testing.

(1) Definition. For purposes of this subsection, the term "security testing" means accessing a computer, computer system, or computer network, solely for the purpose of good faith testing, investigating, or correcting, a security flaw or vulnerability, with the authorization of the owner or operator of such computer, computer system, or computer network.

(2) Permissible acts of security testing. Notwithstanding the provisions of subsection (a)(1)(A), it is not a violation of that subsection for a person to engage in an act of security testing, if such act does not constitute infringement under this title or a violation of applicable law other than this section, including section 1030 of title 18 and those provisions of title 18 amended by the Computer Fraud and Abuse Act of 1986.

(3) Factors in determining exemption. In determining whether a person qualifies for the exemption under paragraph (2), the factors to be considered shall include—

(A) whether the information derived from the security testing was used solely to promote the security of the owner or operator of such computer, computer system or computer network, or shared directly with the developer of such computer, computer system, or computer network; and

(B) whether the information derived from the security testing was used or maintained in a manner that does not facilitate infringement under this title or a violation of applicable law other than this section, including a violation of privacy or breach of security.

(4) Use of technological means for security testing. Notwithstanding the provisions of subsection (a)(2), it is not a violation of that subsection for a person to develop, produce, distribute or employ technological means for the sole purpose of performing the acts of security testing described in subsection (2), provided such technological means does not otherwise violate section (a)(2).

(k) Certain analog devices and certain technological measures.

(1) Certain analog devices.

(A) Effective 18 months after the date of the enactment of this chapter [enacted Oct. 28, 1998], no person shall manufacture, import, offer to the public, provide or otherwise traffic in any—

(i) VHS format analog video cassette recorder unless such recorder conforms to the automatic gain control copy control technology;

(ii) 8mm format analog video cassette camcorder unless such camcorder conforms to the automatic gain control technology;

(iii) Beta format analog video cassette recorder, unless such recorder conforms to the automatic gain control copy control technology, except that this requirement shall not apply until there are 1,000 Beta format analog video cassette recorders sold in the United States in any one calendar year after the date of the enactment of this chapter [enacted Oct. 28, 1998];

(iv) 8mm format analog video cassette recorder that is not an analog video cassette camcorder, unless such recorder conforms to the automatic gain control copy control technology, except that this requirement shall not apply until there are 20,000 such recorders sold in the United States in any one calendar year after the date of the enactment of this chapter [enacted Oct. 28, 1998]; or

(v) analog video cassette recorder that records using an NTSC format video input and that is not otherwise covered under clauses (i) through (iv), unless such device conforms to the automatic gain control copy control technology.

(B) Effective on the date of the enactment of this chapter [enacted Oct. 28, 1998], no person shall manufacture, import, offer to the public, provide or otherwise traffic in—

(i) any VHS format analog video cassette recorder or any 8mm format analog video cassette recorder if the design of the model of such recorder has been modified after such date of enactment so that a model of recorder that previously conformed to the automatic gain control copy control technology no longer conforms to such technology; or

(ii) any VHS format analog video cassette recorder, or any 8mm format analog video cassette recorder that is not an 8mm analog video cassette camcorder, if the design of the model of such recorder has been modified after such date of enactment so that a model of recorder that previously conformed to the four-line colorstripe copy control technology no longer conforms to such technology.

Manufacturers that have not previously manufactured or sold a VHS format analog video cassette recorder, or an 8mm format analog cassette recorder, shall be required to conform to the four-line colorstripe copy control technology in the initial model of any such recorder manufactured after the date of the enactment of this chapter [enacted Oct. 28, 1998], and thereafter to continue conforming to the four-line colorstripe copy control technology. For purposes of this subparagraph, an analog video cassette recorder "conforms to" the four-line colorstripe copy control technology if it records a signal that, when played back by the playback function of that recorder in the normal viewing mode, exhibits, on a reference display device, a display containing distracting visible lines through portions of the viewable picture.

(2) Certain encoding restrictions. No person shall apply the automatic gain control copy control technology or colorstripe copy control technology to prevent or limit consumer copying except such copying—

(A) of a single transmission, or specified group of transmissions, of live events or of audiovisual works for which a member of the public has exercised choice in selecting the transmissions, including the content of the transmissions or the time of receipt of such transmissions, or both, and as to which such member is charged a separate fee for each such transmission or specified group of transmissions;

(B) from a copy of a transmission of a live event or an audiovisual work if such transmission is provided by a channel or service where payment is made by a member of the public for such channel or service in the form of a subscription fee that entitles the member of the public to receive all of the programming contained in such channel or service;

(C) from a physical medium containing one or more prerecorded audiovisual works; or

(D) from a copy of a transmission described in subparagraph (A) or from a copy made from a physical medium described in subparagraph (C).

In the event that a transmission meets both the conditions set forth in subparagraph (A) and those set forth in subparagraph (B), the transmission shall be treated as a transmission described in subparagraph (A).

(3) Inapplicability. This subsection shall not—

(A) require any analog video cassette camcorder to conform to the automatic gain control copy control technology with respect to any video signal received through a camera lens;

(B) apply to the manufacture, importation, offer for sale, provision of, or other trafficking in, any professional analog video cassette recorder; or

(C) apply to the offer for sale or provision of, or other trafficking in, any previously owned analog video cassette recorder, if such recorder was legally manufactured and sold when new and not subsequently modified in violation of paragraph (1)(B).

(4) Definitions. For purposes of this subsection:

(A) An "analog video cassette recorder" means a device that records, or a device that includes a function that records, on electromagnetic tape in an analog format the electronic impulses produced by the video and audio portions of a television program, motion picture, or other form of audiovisual work.

(B) An "analog video cassette camcorder" means an analog video cassette recorder that contains a recording function that operates through a camera lens and through a video input that may be connected with a television or other video playback device.

(C) An analog video cassette recorder "conforms" to the automatic gain control copy control technology if it—

(i) detects one or more of the elements of such technology and does not record the motion picture or transmission protected by such technology; or

(ii) records a signal that, when played back, exhibits a meaningfully distorted or degraded display.

(D) The term "professional analog video cassette recorder" means an analog video cassette recorder that is designed, manufactured, marketed, and intended for use by a person who regularly employs such a device for a lawful business or industrial use, including making, performing, displaying, distributing, or transmitting copies of motion pictures on a commercial scale.

(E) The terms "VHS format," "8mm format," "Beta format," "automatic gain control copy control technology," "colorstripe copy control technology," "four-line version of the colorstripe copy control technology," and "NTSC" have the meanings that are commonly understood in the consumer electronics and motion picture industries as of the date of the enactment of this chapter [enacted Oct. 28, 1998].

(5) Violations. Any violation of paragraph (1) of this subsection shall be treated as a violation of subsection (b)(1) of this section. Any violation of paragraph (2) of this subsection shall be deemed an "act of circumvention" for the purposes of section 1203(c)(3)(A) of this chapter.

Bibliography

Badgley, Robert. "Internet Domain Names and ICANN Arbitration: The Emerging 'Law' of Domain Name Custody Disputes." *Texas Review of Law and Policy* 5 (2001): 343.

Benkler, Yochai. "Free as the Air to Common Use: First Amendment Constraints on Enclosure of the Public Domain." *New York University Law Review* 74 (1999): 354.

Calabresi, Guido and Jeffrey O. Cooper. "New Directions in Tort Law." *Valparaiso University Law Review* 30 (1996): 859.

Dinwoodie, Graeme B. "A New Copyright Order: Why National Courts Should Create Global Norms." *University of Pennsylvania Law Review* 149 (2000): 469.

Exon, Susan Nauss. "A New Shoe Is Needed to Walk Through Cyberspace Jurisdiction." *Albany Law Journal of Science and Technology* 11 (2000): 1.

Freeman, Bradley J. and Robert J. C. Deane. "Trademarks and the Internet: A Canadian Perspective." *University of British Columbia Law Review* 34 (2001): 345.

Fulda, Joseph S. "Data Mining and Privacy." *Albany Law Journal of Science and Technology* 11 (2000): 105.

Gimbel, Mark. "Note, Some Thoughts on the Implications of Trusted Systems for Intellectual Property Law." *Stanford Law Review* 50 (1998) 1671.

Ginsburg, Jane C. "Copyright and Control over New Technologies of Dissemination." *Columbia Law Review* 101 (2001): 1613.

Gore, Stephanie. "Eureka! But I Filed too Late . . . : The Harm/Benefit Dichotomy of a First-to-File Patent System." *University of Chicago Law School Roundtable* (1993): 293.

Harper, Fowler V. and Fleming James, Jr. *The Law of Torts* §§ 101-04 (2d ed. 1996).

Johnson-Laird, Andy. "Symposium: Copyright Owners' Rights And Users' Privileges on the Internet: The Anatomy of the Internet Meets the Body of the Law." *Dayton Law Review* 22 (1997): 465.

Kotzun, Shandra J. "The Digital Millennium Copyright Act: Anticircumvention Ban Gives More Rights to Copyright Owners." *Tulane Journal of Technology and Intellectual Property* 3 (2001): 117.

Kramarsky, Stephen M. "Copyright Enforcement in the Internet Age: The Law and Technology of Digital Rights Management." *Journal of Art and Entertainment Law* 11 (2001): 1.

Leaffer, Marshall A. "The New World of International Trademark Law." *Marquette Intellectual Property Law Review* 2 (1998): 1.

Lemley, Mark A. and Eugene Volokh. "Freedom of Speech and Injunctions in Intellectual Property Cases." *Duke Law Journal* 48 (1998): 147

McCarthy, J. Thomas. McCarthy on Trademarks & Unfair Competition § 17:25-27 (4th ed. 1998).

Merges, Robert P. "Commercial Success and Patent Standards: Economic Perspectives on Innovation." *California Law Review* 76 (1988): 805.

Merges, Robert P. and Richard R. Nelson. "On the Complex Economics of Patent Scope." *Columbia Law Review* 90 (1990): 839.

Najarian, David C. "Internet Domains and Trademark Claims: First Amendment Considerations." *Journal of Law and Technology* 41 (2001): 127.

Nimmer, David. "A Riff on Fair Use in the Digital Millennium Copyright Act." *University of Pennsylvania Law Review* 148 (2000): 673.

Patterson, L. Ray. "Copyright in the New Millennium: Resolving the Conflict Between Property Rights and Political Rights." *Ohio State Law Journal* 62 (2001): 703.

Paylago, U. "Trademark Infringement, Meta-tags, and the Initial Interest Confusion Remedy." *Media Law and Policy* 9 (2000): 49.

Post, Robert. "Encryption Source Code and the First Amendment." *Berkeley Technology Law Journal* 15 (2000): 713.

Raysman, Richard and Peter Brown. "Recent Linking Issues." *New York Law Journal* (Feb. 8, 2000): 3.

Rotunda, Ronald D. and John E. Nowak. *Treatise on Constitutional Law* § 20.5 (1999).

Sack, Robert D. *Sack on Defamation* § 1.2.4 (3d ed. 1999).

Scassa, Teresa. "Text and Context: Making Sense of Canada's New Personal Information Protection Legislation." *Ottawa Law Review* 32 (2000/2001): 1.

Scheindlin, Shira A. and Jeffrey Rabkin. "Electronic Discovery in Federal Civil Litigation: Is Rule 34 Up to the Task?" *British Columbia Law Review* 34 (2000): 327.

Siebrasse, Norman A. "Property Rights Theory of the Limits of Copyright." *University of Toronto Law Journal* 51 (2001): 1.

Simon, Lori E. "Appellations of Origin: The Continuing Controversy." *Journal of International Law Business* 5 (1983): 132.

Smith, Bradford L. "The Third Industrial Revolution: Policymaking for the Internet." *Columbia. Science and Technology Law Review* 3 (2001): 1.

Stefik, Mark. "Shifting the Possible: How Trusted Systems and Digital Property Rights Challenge Us to Rethink Digital Publishing." *Berkeley Technology Law Journal.* 12 (1997): 137.

"Symposium Beyond Napster: Debating the Future of Copyright on the Internet: Keynote Address: Resolving Tensions Between Copyright and the Internet." *American University Law Review* (2000): 409.

Travis, Hannibal. "Comment, Pirates of the Information Infrastructure: Blackstonian Copyright and the First Amendment." *Berkeley Technology Law Journal* 15 (2000): 777.

Weiser, Philip J. "Internet Governance, Standard Setting, and Self-Regulation." *Northern Kentucky Law Review* 28 (2001): 822.

WIPO Copyright Treaty, Apr. 12, 1997, Art. 11, S. Treaty Doc. No. 105-17 (1997)

Index

About the Authors

Leopoldo Brandt Graterol is a Venezuelan attorney who graduated from the Andrés Bello Catholic (UCAB) University Law School in Caracas, Venezuela, in 1988, and obtained a master's degree in comparative jurisprudence from the University of Texas at Austin School of Law in 1991. His practice is mainly corporate law and cyberspace issues. He is founder and teacher of the E-commerce Law Seminar at the UCAB University Law School in Caracas Venezuela, the first seminar in its class in Venezuela. He is also an international associate of the American Bar Association. Mr. Brandt has attended several e-commerce-related courses and online seminars. He is a co-founder and legal coordinator of the Venezuelan Chamber of E-commerce (Cavecom-e) and Coordinator of the E-Commerce and Digital Signature Legislative Process in Venezuela. He is a member of ICANN Membership Task Force for Latin America and Caribbean. Mr. Brandt is a columnist on technology and e-commerce-related matters for the renowned Venezuelan Newspaper *El Universal* and its digital version EUD.com, and a collaborator of Latontrade.com. He is senior and managing partner at Azpúrua and Brandt, the leading Internet and e-commerce law boutique in Venezuela. He is also the senior legal counsel of Teleflores.com

John Ng'ang'a Gathegi is an associate professor of information studies and legal informatics at Florida State University and a member of the California Bar. His interests are mainly in the area of information technology and the law, with a special focus in intellectual property rights on the Internet. He has previously taught information policy as assistant professor at Florida State University and as an adjunct professor at San Jose State University in California. He has also taught legal resources and internet research strategies courses at the City College of San Francisco. Born in Kenya, he moved to the United States, where he obtained several graduate degrees, including a doctor of philosophy degree from the University of California at Berkeley, and a Juris Doctor from Boalt Hall School of Law, also at Berkeley. At Boalt, he was articles editor on the *Berkeley Technology Law Journal*. Following the practice of law in California and prior to returning to Florida, Dr. Gathegi was Dean of the Humanities, Arts and Social Sciences Division at Merritt College in California.